Reasoning and Writing

A Direct Instruction Program

Level F
Teacher's Guide

Siegfried Engelmann

Bonnie Grossen

A Division of The McGraw-Hill Companies

Columbus, Ohio

Cover Credits

(l) Artville, (r) PhotoDisc.

RA/McGraw-Hill

A Division of The McGraw·Hill Companies

Sen
SRA iries to:
8787 y-Hill
Columbace
43240-4027
Printed in
nited States of America.

ISBN 0-02-6...97-3

3 4 5 6 7 8 9
BH 06 05 04 03 02

Contents

Program Summary

Facts about *Reasoning and Writing, Level F*

Students who are appropriately placed in Level F	Students who have completed Level E or who pass the placement criteria for Level F
Placement criteria	Students are able to read on at least a fourth-grade level Students meet placement test criteria for • Copying words at the rate of 15 words per minute • Writing basic paragraphs (See the placement test on page 9.)
Format of lessons	Scripted presentations for all activities Program designed for presentation to entire class
Number of lessons	70~~100~~ (including 7 test lessons)
Scheduled time for language periods	45 minutes per period Usually, one lesson can be completed in each period
Weekly schedule	For presenting Level F in 1 year: 2–3 lessons per week
	For presenting Level F in 1 semester: Daily Lessons
Teacher's material	Teacher's Guide Presentation Book Answer Key Booklet
Student's material	Textbook
In-program tests	Every 10th lesson
Remedies	Specified as part of each test lesson

Scope and Sequence for *Reasoning and Writing, Level F*

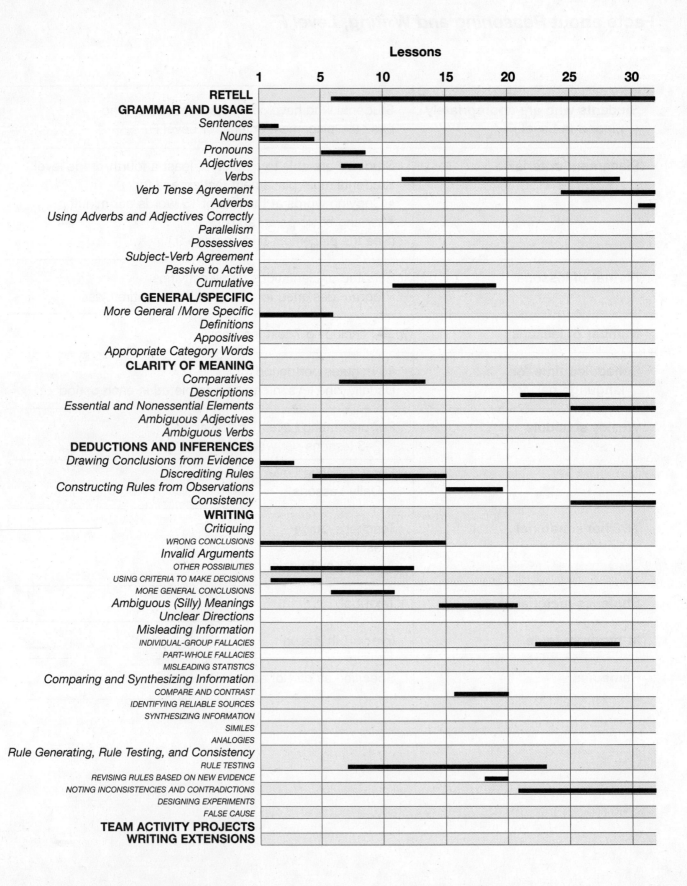

Lessons
1 5 10 15 20 25 30

RETELL

GRAMMAR AND USAGE
Sentences
Nouns
Pronouns
Adjectives
Verbs
Verb Tense Agreement
Adverbs
Using Adverbs and Adjectives Correctly
Parallelism
Possessives
Subject-Verb Agreement
Passive to Active
Cumulative

GENERAL/SPECIFIC
More General /More Specific
Definitions
Appositives
Appropriate Category Words

CLARITY OF MEANING
Comparatives
Descriptions
Essential and Nonessential Elements
Ambiguous Adjectives
Ambiguous Verbs

DEDUCTIONS AND INFERENCES
Drawing Conclusions from Evidence
Discrediting Rules
Constructing Rules from Observations
Consistency

WRITING
Critiquing
WRONG CONCLUSIONS
Invalid Arguments
OTHER POSSIBILITIES
USING CRITERIA TO MAKE DECISIONS
MORE GENERAL CONCLUSIONS
Ambiguous (Silly) Meanings
Unclear Directions
Misleading Information
INDIVIDUAL-GROUP FALLACIES
PART-WHOLE FALLACIES
MISLEADING STATISTICS
Comparing and Synthesizing Information
COMPARE AND CONTRAST
IDENTIFYING RELIABLE SOURCES
SYNTHESIZING INFORMATION
SIMILES
ANALOGIES
Rule Generating, Rule Testing, and Consistency
RULE TESTING
REVISING RULES BASED ON NEW EVIDENCE
NOTING INCONSISTENCIES AND CONTRADICTIONS
DESIGNING EXPERIMENTS
FALSE CAUSE
TEAM ACTIVITY PROJECTS
WRITING EXTENSIONS

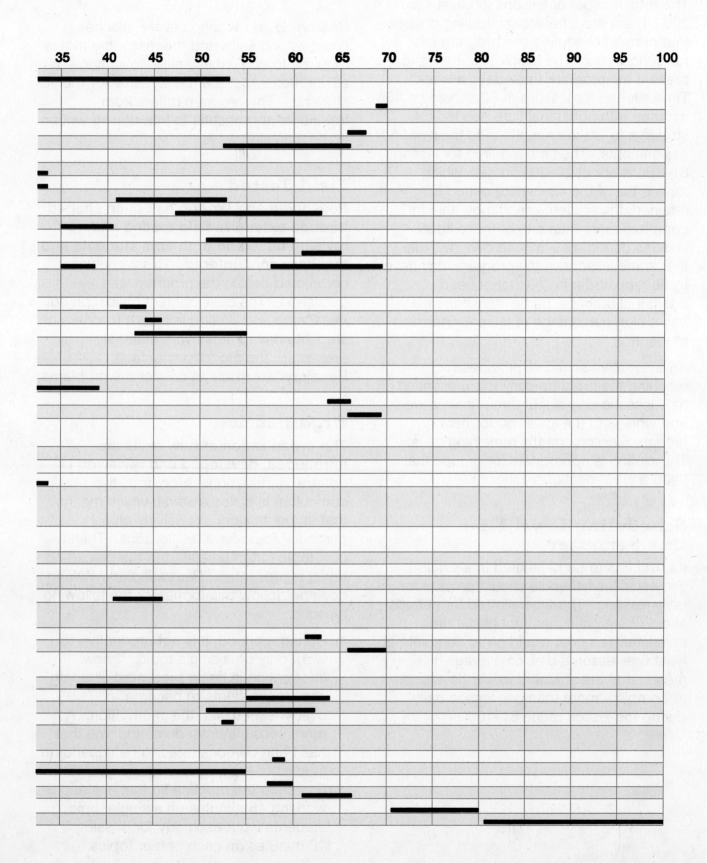

Scheduling Level F for One Year

The total number of lessons in Level F is 100. There are different scheduling options that permit scheduling this program over a full school year. The simplest option is to present the program three days a week. Time allotted for lessons 1–80 should be 45 minutes with additional time needed for students to make corrections to their writing assignments. The time required for lessons 81–100 is about 20–30 minutes, which means that if the 45–minute period is retained, the students should be able to complete more than one of these later lessons during a 45–minute period. Note that some lessons in the program may have to be repeated for groups that need additional practice, particularly if the class has a high percentage of lower-performing students.

An alternative schedule provides for teaching the program daily but presenting new lessons only about three times a week and work with the lower-performers on repeated lessons on the remaining days. This option is appropriate for groups that need a great deal of practice

Scheduling Level F for One Semester

If Level F is to be presented in a single semester the schedule should provide for daily lessons. The time allotted for periods should be 45 minutes throughout the semester. The goal would be to complete at least one lesson a day, on average, which means that the students would be expected to complete more than one lesson daily during the lesson range 81–100.

How the Program Is Different

Reasoning and Writing Level F teaches basic writing skills and the reasoning that is required to apply these skills to writing assignments that are manageable for the students. The program differs from traditional approaches to introducing writing in the following ways:

Field Tested

Reasoning and Writing has been shaped through extensive field testing and revising based on problems students and teachers encountered. This work was completed before the program was published. The development philosophy of *Reasoning and Writing* is that, if teachers or students have trouble with material presented, the program is at fault. Revisions are made to correct the problems.

Organization

The organization of how skills are introduced, developed and reviewed is unique. In traditional programs, the curriculum is called a spiral, which means that students work exclusively on a particular topic for a few lessons. Then a new topic (often unrelated to the preceding topic) is presented. *Reasoning and Writing* does not follow this format for the following reasons:

a) During a period, it is not productive to work only on a single topic. If new information is being presented, it is very easy for students to become overwhelmed with the information. A more sensible procedure, and one that has been demonstrated to be superior in studies of learning and memory, is to distribute the practice so that, instead of working 45 minutes on a single topic, students work each day for possibly 10 minutes on each of four topics.

b) When full-period topics are presented, it becomes very difficult for the teacher to provide practice on the latest skills taught. Unless the skills taught are used and reviewed, student performance will deteriorate, and the skills will have to be retaught when they again appear. A more sensible organization is to present work on skills continuously (not discontinuously), so that students work on a particular topic (such as pronoun clarity) for part of 15 or 20 lessons, not for 5 or 6 entire lessons at a time. In this context of continuous development of skills, review becomes automatic, and reteaching becomes unnecessary because students use the skills in almost every lesson.

c) When skills are not developed continuously, students are expected to learn a lot of new concepts during a short period and are also expected to become "automatic" in applying the new concepts and skills. For most students, adequate learning will not occur. A more sensible way is to develop skills and concepts in small steps, so that students are not required to learn as much new material at a time, which means they receive a sufficient amount of practice to become facile or automatic in applying what they learn.

d) When skills are not developed continuously students and teachers may develop very negative attitudes about mastery. Students often learn that they are not expected to "learn" the new material because it will go away in a few days. Teachers become frustrated because they often understand that students need a lot more practice, but they are unable to provide it and at the same time move through the program at a reasonable rate. Again, the continuous development of skills solves this problem because students learn very quickly that what is presented is used in this lesson, in the next lesson, and so forth. When the practice is sufficient, students

develop the mind-set or expectation needed for learning a skill to mastery because it is something they will need in the immediate future.

e) When lessons are not clearly related to periods of time, the teacher has no precise way to gauge the performance of the students or to judge how long to spend on a particular lesson. A more reasonable procedure is to organize material into lessons, each requiring so much time to teach. The teacher then knows that the lesson has the potential of teaching students within a class period of 45 minutes.

f) The focus of *Reasoning and Writing* is on writing; however, students need various skills to write acceptably. These skills are taught in isolation (or in a simple form that provides students with lots of practice) and are then funneled into more complex applications. The skills that are taught are organized in *tracks.* A track is an ongoing development of a particular topic. Within each lesson, work from three to six tracks is presented. The teaching presentations are designed so it is possible to present the entire lesson in 45 minutes (although some lessons may be shorter and others may require more time for lower performers).

From lesson to lesson, the work on new skills develops a small step at a time so that students are not overwhelmed with new information and receive enough practice both to master skills and to become facile with them. Students, therefore, learn quickly about *learning new concepts* and realize that what they are learning has utility because they will use it.

Emphasis of Level F

Although the tracks presented in Level F develop specific skills in usage, grammar, identifying problems with arguments, and following particular formats for expressing ideas, the program teaches **thinking—**

higher-order thinking. Within this broad domain, the program has recurring emphases that are particularly relevant to the student who is learning to think critically. These emphases cut across the various tracks and various exercises. They are **alternative explanations, parallelism, general versus specific,** and **the relationship between a large population and a sample of members.**

ALTERNATIVE EXPLANATIONS

The recurring message conveyed to the students is that simply because arguments and accounts appear in writing does not mean that they are valid or without fault. An argument may draw a conclusion that is apparently reasonable, but may not be the only conclusion that derives from the evidence. By showing another possible conclusion, the student demonstrates that the original argument is faulty. Similarly, when students rewrite directions for making a figure so the directions will have fewer sentences and fewer words, the students are showing an alternative, which suggests that the original directions were adequate but were not necessarily the best or the only ones possible.

Students work various problems that require them to use the information provided in an argument or a situation to write something different from what the account shown in the exercise indicated. Students also rewrite directions and reorder information to show alternatives that are at least as acceptable as the original and that may challenge the implication that the original is either superior or exclusive.

PARALLELISM

Parallelism is very important in writing and in thinking. Just as there are different situations that are parallel to the extent that the situations may be examples of a false cause or an unwarranted opinion, there are parallel ways to describe these situations. Level F presents exercises that require

students to respond to an assertion by using a parallel sentence. An assertion might be:

Doing situps is the only way to strengthen your abdominal muscles.

The negation:

No, swimming and wrestling are also ways to strengthen your abdominal muscles.

Parallelism is important in parts of speech. Specifically, statements may be transformed into questions that use all the same words. In such questions, the various words have the same functions and have the same parts of speech as they have in the corresponding statements. For instance:

That bus does move fast.

The parallel question:

Does that bus move fast?

If the student knows the parts of speech in the statement, the student knows the parts of speech in the question.

The broad application of parallelism has to do with generating a parallel form that is familiar. A general rule of grammar is that parallel parts have the same position and function and the same part of speech. If they are in the predicate of a sentence, they are in the predicate of the parallel sentence. For example:

She asked a question.

The words **a question** are the object of a transitive verb (**asked**). In the parallel sentence:

She asked what she was supposed to do.

The words that are parallel to **a question** are also the object of a transitive verb.

Not only does this orientation to grammar permit students to experiment and learn the limits of the parts of speech and categories (such as object of the verb), the orientation also becomes closely related to the notion of providing alternative explanations. Students can learn a lot about the range of things that are labeled **adjective** by replacing the adjective in this sentence:

She listened to long _____ lectures.

The range of replacements includes words that look like verbs (**tiring, exciting**), units that have more than one word (**half-hour**). and words that seem to be nouns (**science**). All are adjectives because all occupy the same position and have the same function.

GENERAL VERSUS SPECIFIC

The third theme that runs through exercises in Level F is general versus specific. These are key notions to higher-order thinking and, like parallelism, they may occur in contexts that involve alternative explanations. Both general and specific play an important role in writing. A summary is a statement that is **general.** Just as the summary has an organizing function, the headings of a traditional outline have such a function. The heading **physical characteristics** provides a general structure for organizing information about a place.

General statements may be appropriate in other contexts. A general statement is needed as a part of the evidence in a simple deduction. A more-general statement, however, cannot occur in the conclusion. This argument is faulty because the conclusion is more general than the statements in the evidence:

John comes from Calhoun County. John is a slob. So everybody from Calhoun County must be a slob.

An appropriate argument would have the more general statement in the evidence. In Level F, students identify the problem with deductions of this type. They also work

with directions that are too general. For example:

Make two lines that touch each other.

Those directions could tell a person how to make the letter **T**; however, they could also tell how to make other letters (**L**, **V**). As directions for making the letter **T**, therefore, the directions are too general. The test for whether an explanation or a set of directions is too general is: "Can the explanation or directions lead to a class of possibilities that is too large?" If directions are designed for someone to make only the letter **T**, the directions above are too general.

Students compare sentences with respect to how general or specific the sentences are, and they create sentences that are either more specific or more general than a given sentence. For example, students start with this sentence:

He touched a black triangle.

They write a sentence that is more general and one that is more specific. (He touched a triangle. He touched a small black triangle.)

Students also write critiques of too-general directions for making figures. They first indicate why the directions are too general. The reason is that if somebody followed those directions, that person could respond to more than one possible figure. Students explain the ambiguities, then indicate what clear directions would say.

RELATIONSHIP BETWEEN POPULATION AND SAMPLE

The fourth theme is that a sample population may provide a distorted idea of the range of variation in the whole population. If a person visited a strange island and observed 14 creatures of a type never before observed, the person might construct rules that are valid for this sample; however, these rules might not be valid for a larger sample. The "population" theme develops in several directions. The first has to do with indicating fair tests of rules that are based on a small sample. How many observations are reasonable? What kind of information would discredit the original rule? What kind of information would support the original rule?

Another direction has to do with making numbers lie and critiquing arguments that are guilty of creating distortions by using questionable statistical information. Students are not exposed to complicated mathematics for dealing with larger populations; however, they indicate possible problems with arguments that apparently make numbers lie. For example, a person measures the height of 26 10-year-old children and concludes that, on the average, the boys are taller than the girls. The basis for this conclusion is that in the sample, 3 out of the tallest 4 children are boys. To discredit the evidence this argument uses, students construct a population of 26 children in which 3 of the tallest 4 children are boys; however, the population clearly shows that the girls are, on the average, taller than the boys.

Note that students not only identify the problems, they write about them. They use the same evidence but draw a conclusion that is as reasonable as the conclusion drawn by the original argument.

Similar exercises provide students with practice viewing conclusions skeptically and considering alternatives that are consistent with the evidence given but that lead to a different conclusion. With this framework for viewing arguments, students have a good beginning in understanding what scientific method is really about—rules that are consistent with what we know about the world. However, as our information about the world increases, we are provided with a basis for more specific rules, often rules that contradict those that were earlier valid.

Placement

Level F is appropriate for students in fifth to eighth grade who read on at least a fourth-grade level. Level F is designed for two different populations: students who have completed *Reasoning and Writing, Level E,* and students who have not gone through any earlier levels of *Reasoning and Writing*. For students who have completed E, the program provides a new slant on some of the things that they have already done—new variations in outline diagrams, new exercise types that relate to familiar topics like specific and general, and new grammar topics.

For students who are new to *Reasoning and Writing,* the program provides sufficient instruction to teach the various writing and analytical skills. Qualified students are those who pass the placement test. These students should have some knowledge of writing and punctuating sentences and should be able to read reasonably well. The placement test provides a rough indication of whether students should be placed in Level F. Administer the placement test to students who haven't gone through earlier levels of *Reasoning and Writing*.

A reproducible copy of the test appears on page 9. The test is group administered and requires about 10 minutes for students to complete. Directions for presenting the test begin on page 10.

Name: _____   Date: _____

PART 1

Each item begins with a capital and ends with a period, but some of the items are not sentences and should not be punctuated the way they are shown. Write the number of each item that is a sentence.

1. They talked.
2. Before school opened the other morning.
3. Under the stairs and running around the basement.
4. Timmy hit the baseball.
5. In the evening, the bugs came out.
6. Why Fred could not have gone to the meeting.
7. How I met my best friend.
8. Make a circle that is one inch across.
9. Sit down.
10. His statement indicated that he didn't see the accident.

PART 2

Rewrite the passage. The number after each period tells the number of changes you must make.

Jan collected butterflies some was small and some was large. (5)
She told her friends that she were going to catch a rare pink butterfly
and she went out with a net and she came back with four butterflies. (5)

PART 3

This description tells about more than one of the figures. Write the letter of each figure that fits the description.

Description: The square is about 1 inch long on each side. A dot is in the middle of the top line. A small b is directly above the dot.

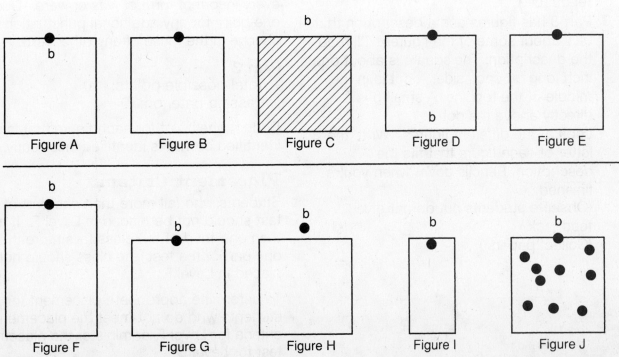

Figure A   Figure B   Figure C   Figure D   Figure E

Figure F   Figure G   Figure H   Figure I   Figure J

Administering the Test

Reproduce copies of the test. Pass out a test and a piece of lined paper to each student. Direct students to write their name on the lined paper. Present the directions below:

1. Find part 1.
   - Some of these items are sentences. Some are not. All the items begin with a capital and end with a period, but don't be fooled. Not all of them are sentences.
   - Write the number of each item that is a sentence. Don't write the numbers for the items that are not sentences. Pencils down when you're finished. (Observe students but do not give feedback.)
2. Part 2 shows a passage that is not written well. After each period, there's a number that tells how many mistakes were made.
   - You're going to rewrite the passage so it has no mistakes. Write clear sentences. Don't change anything in the original passage unless it is a mistake. Pencils down when you've written the passage so it has no mistakes. (Observe students but do not give feedback.)
3. Part 3 has figures and a description that tells about some of the figures. I'll read the description: The square is about one inch long on each side. A dot is in the middle of the top line. A small b is directly above the dot.
   - Look at the different figures. Write the letter of each figure that fits the description. Pencils down when you're finished. (Observe students but do not give feedback.)
   - (Collect papers.)

Scoring the Test

Key:
Part 1: 1, 4, 5, 8, 9, 10.
Part 2: Check only that underlined, bold-faced parts are correct.

Jan collected butterflies. **S**ome were small, and some **were** large. She told her friends that she **was** going to catch a rare pink butterfly. **S**he went out with a net. **S**he came back with four butterflies OR. . . .with a net **and came** back with four butterflies.

(underlined/numbered markings: butterflies**.** (1) **S**ome (2) / **were** (3) small**,** (4) **were** (5) / **was** (6) / butterfly**.** (7) **S**he (8) / net**.** (9) **S**he (10) / **and came** (9))

Part 3: E, G, J

PART 1
Total possible points: 12
Passing criterion: 8

Score two points for every correct item; deduct two points for every non-sentence listed.

PART 2
Total possible points: 10
Passing criterion: 7

Start with a score of 10. Deduct one point for each period or capital that does not correspond to the key. Deduct one point for every incorrect form of *was* or *were*. Deduct one point for any additional punctuation or change in the tense of any other verb.

PART 3
Total possible points: 10
Passing criterion: 9

Deduct one point for each figure that is not identified or that is identified incorrectly.

Placement Criteria

Students who fail more than one part of the test should not be placed in Level F. If more than one-third of the class fails more than one part of the test, the class should not be placed in Level F.

To determine appropriate placement for students who do not meet the placement criteria for Level F, administer the placement test for Level D.

Teaching the Program

Level F is designed to be presented to the entire class. You should generally be able to teach one lesson during a 45-minute period. All writing assignments are completed during this period.

Classroom Arrangement

Arrange seating so you can receive very quick information on high performers and low performers. A good plan is to organize the students something like this:

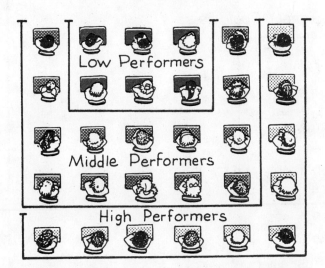

Front of Classroom

Low Performers

Middle Performers

High Performers

The lowest performers are closest to the front of the classroom. Middle performers are arranged around the lowest performers. Highest performers are arranged around the periphery. With this arrangement, you can position yourself so that, by taking a few steps during the time that students are working, you can sample low, average and high performers.

While different variations of this arrangement are possible, be careful not to seat low performers far from the front-center of the room. The highest performers, understandably, can be farthest from the center because they attend better, learn faster, and need less observation and feedback.

Teaching

When you teach the program, a basic rule is that you should not present from the front of the room. For nearly all activities, you direct work-specified tasks. You should present from somewhere in the middle of the room (in no set place); and as students work, you should move around and quickly observe a good sample of students. Although you won't be able to observe every student working every task, you can observe at least a dozen in a couple of minutes.

Rehearse the lesson before presenting it to the class. Don't simply read the text—act it out. Watch your wording. If you rehearse the early lessons before presenting them, you'll soon learn how to present efficiently from the script.

In later lessons, you should scan the list of skills at the beginning of each lesson. New skills are in boldface type. If a new skill is introduced in a lesson, rehearse it. Most activities in the lesson will not be new but will be a variation of what you've presented earlier, so you may not need to rehearse these activities.

Using the Teacher Presentation Scripts

The scripts specify how to present all activities in a lesson. The first part of the period involves work on skills, the second part on writing.

The script for each lesson indicates precisely how to present each structured activity. The script shows what you say, what you do, and what the student responses should be.

What you say appears in blue type:

You say this.

What you do appears in parentheses:

(You do this.)

The responses of the students are in italics:

Students say this.

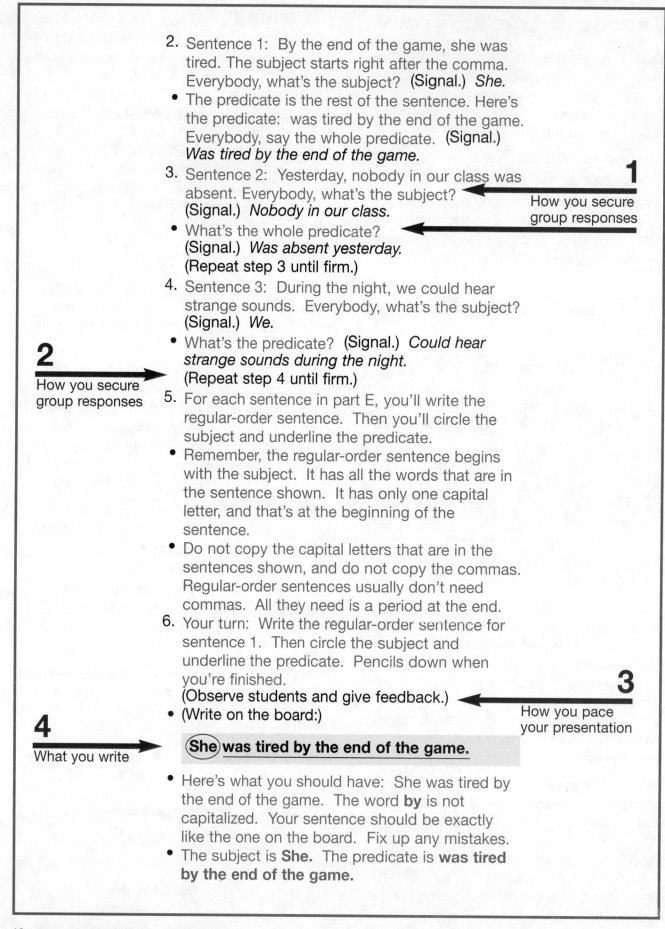

2. Sentence 1: By the end of the game, she was tired. The subject starts right after the comma. Everybody, what's the subject? **(Signal.)** *She.*
   - The predicate is the rest of the sentence. Here's the predicate: was tired by the end of the game. Everybody, say the whole predicate. **(Signal.)** *Was tired by the end of the game.*
3. Sentence 2: Yesterday, nobody in our class was absent. Everybody, what's the subject? **(Signal.)** *Nobody in our class.*

1
How you secure
group responses

   - What's the whole predicate? **(Signal.)** *Was absent yesterday.*
   (Repeat step 3 until firm.)
4. Sentence 3: During the night, we could hear strange sounds. Everybody, what's the subject? **(Signal.)** *We.*
   - What's the predicate? **(Signal.)** *Could hear strange sounds during the night.*
   (Repeat step 4 until firm.)

2

How you secure
group responses

5. For each sentence in part E, you'll write the regular-order sentence. Then you'll circle the subject and underline the predicate.
   - Remember, the regular-order sentence begins with the subject. It has all the words that are in the sentence shown. It has only one capital letter, and that's at the beginning of the sentence.
   - Do not copy the capital letters that are in the sentences shown, and do not copy the commas. Regular-order sentences usually don't need commas. All they need is a period at the end.
6. Your turn: Write the regular-order sentence for sentence 1. Then circle the subject and underline the predicate. Pencils down when you're finished.
   (Observe students and give feedback.)

3

How you pace
your presentation

   - (Write on the board:)

4
What you write

   (She) was tired by the end of the game.

   - Here's what you should have: She was tired by the end of the game. The word **by** is not capitalized. Your sentence should be exactly like the one on the board. Fix up any mistakes.
   - The subject is **She.** The predicate is **was tired by the end of the game.**

Follow the specified wording in the script. While wording variations from the specified script are not always dangerous, you will be assured of communicating clearly with the students if you follow the script exactly. The reason is that the wording is controlled, and the tasks are arranged so they provide succinct wording and focus clearly on important aspects of what the students are to do. Although you may at first feel uncomfortable "reading" from a script (and you may feel that the students will not pay attention), follow the scripts very closely; try to present them as if you were saying something important to the students. If you do, you'll find after a while that working from a script is not difficult and that students indeed respond well to what you say.

A sample script appears on page 12.

The arrows show the four different things that you'll do when you present the script. You'll make sure that group responses involve all the students. You'll also "firm" critical parts of the exercises. And you'll use information based on what the students are doing to judge whether you'll proceed quickly or wait a few more seconds before moving on with the presentation.

ARROW 1: GROUP RESPONSES

Some of the tasks call for group responses. If students respond in unison, you receive good information about whether "most" of the students are performing correctly. The simplest way to signal students to respond together is to adopt a timing practice—just like the timing in a musical piece.

Step 3 presents a task that students respond to in unison.

3. Sentence 2. Yesterday, nobody in our class was absent. Everybody, what's the subject? (Signal.) *Nobody in our class.*

You can signal when students are to respond by nodding, clapping one time, snapping your fingers or tapping your foot. After initially establishing the timing for signals, you can signal through voice inflection only.

Students will not be able to initiate responses together at the appropriate rate unless you follow these rules:

a) Talk first. Pause a standard length of time (possibly 1 second); then signal. Students are to respond on your signal—not after it or before it.

b) Model responses that are paced reasonably. Don't permit students to produce slow, droney responses. These are dangerous because they rob you of the information that can be derived from appropriate group responses. When students respond in a droney way, many of them are copying responses of others. If students are required to respond at a reasonable speaking rate, all students must initiate responses. Therefore, it's relatively easy to determine which students are not responding and which are saying the wrong thing.

(**Note:** Do not respond with the students unless you are trying to work with them on a difficult response. You present only what's in blue. You do not say the answers with the students, and you should not move your lips or give other spurious clues about what the answer is.)

Think of unison responses this way: If you use them correctly, they provide you with much diagnostic information. They suggest whether you should repeat a task (because the response was weak). They permit you to get information about which students may need more help. They are therefore important early in the program. After students have learned the game, the students will be able to respond on cue with no signal. That will happen, however, only if you always keep a constant time interval between the completion of what you say and your signal.

ARROW 2: FIRMING

When students make mistakes, you correct them. A correction may occur during any part of the teacher presentation that calls for students to respond. Here are the rules for corrections:

- You correct a mistake as soon as you hear it.
- A mistake on oral responses is saying the wrong thing or not responding.

In step 4, students may not say anything or may not correctly answer the question, "What's the subject?" You correct as soon as you hear the mistake. You do not wait until students finish responding before correcting.

To correct, say the correct response and then repeat the task they missed.

> Teacher: During the night, we could hear strange sounds. Everybody, what's the subject? (Signal.)
> Some students: *We could . . .*
> Teacher: The subject is **we.** Listen: During the night, we could hear strange sounds. What's the subject? (Signal.)
> *We*

Remember, wherever there's an oral task that involves all the students, there's a place where students may make mistakes.

Sometimes one step in the exercise involves a series of oral tasks.

> 4. Sentence 3: During the night, we could hear strange sounds. Everybody, what's the subject? (Signal.) *We.*
> - What's the predicate? (Signal.) *Could hear strange sounds during the night.* (Repeat step 4 until firm.)

After correcting any mistakes within this series of tasks, you would return to the beginning of step 4 and present the entire step.

The note **(Repeat step until firm)** occurs when students must correctly produce a series of responses. When you "repeat until firm," you follow these steps:

1) Correct the mistake. (Tell the answer and repeat the task that was missed.)
2) Return to the beginning of the specified step and present the entire step.

"Repeating until firm" provides information you need about the students. When the students made the mistake, you told the answer. Did they remember the answer? Would they now be able to perform the step correctly? The repeat-until-firm procedure provides you with answers to these questions. You present the context in which the mistake occurred, and the students can show you through their responses whether or not the correction worked, whether or not they are **firm.**

The repeat-until-firm direction appears only on the most critical parts of new teaching exercises. It usually focuses on knowledge that is very important for later work. In the activity on page 12, for instance, you want to make sure that the students understand how to identify the part that names. However, if you're quite sure that the mistake was a "glitch" and does not mean that the students lack understanding, don't follow the repeat-until-firm direction.

The specified responses for some tasks are not what some students might say. Expect variability on some group responses. Accept any reasonable wording.

If you want to hold students to the wording that is in the script (which is not necessary for tasks that can be reasonably answered in other ways), say something like, "That's right." Then say the response you want. "Everybody, say it that way."

As a rule, if more than one answer is possible for the task you presented and you know that the students' answers are reasonable, don't bother with a correction. Just move on to the next part of the teacher script.

ARROW 3: PACING YOUR PRESENTATION

You should pace your verbal presentation at a normal speaking rate—as if you were telling somebody something important.

The most typical mistake teachers make is going too slowly or talking as if to preschoolers.

The arrow for number 3 on the diagram shows a way to pace your presentation for activities where students write. The **(Observe students and give feedback)** direction implies a more elaborate response. You sample more students, work and you give feedback, not only to individual students, but also to the group. Here are the basic rules for what to do and what not to do when you observe and give feedback.

1) Make sure that you are not at the front of the class when you present the directions for tasks that involve observing student performance. When you direct students to write a sentence, move from the front of the room to a place where you can quickly sample the performance of low, middle and high performers.

2) As soon as students start to work, start observing. As you observe, make comments to the whole class. Focus these comments on students who are (a) following directions, (b) working quickly, and (c) working accurately. "Wow, a couple of students are almost finished. I haven't seen one mistake so far."

3) When students raise their hand to indicate that they are finished, acknowledge them. (When you acknowledge that they are finished, they are to put their hand down.)

4) If you observe mistakes, do *not* provide a great deal of individual help. Point out any mistakes, but do not do the work for the students. Point to the problem and say, "I think you made a mistake. Look at the first word in your sentence." If students are not following instructions

that you gave, tell them, "You're supposed to circle the subject. You have to listen very carefully to the instructions."

5) Do not wait for the slowest students to complete the activities before presenting the work check (during which students correct their work and fix up any mistakes). A good rule early in the program is to allow a **reasonable amount of time** for students to complete their work. You can usually use the middle performers as a gauge for what is reasonable. As you observe that they are completing their work, announce, "Okay, you have about 10 seconds more to finish up." At the end of that time, continue in the exercise.

6) Circulate among the students and make sure that they fix up any mistakes you identify.

7) If you observe a serious problem that is not unique to only the lowest performers, tell the class, "Stop. We seem to have a serious problem." Repeat the part of the exercise that gives them information about what they are to do. (**Note:** Do not provide "new teaching." Simply repeat the part of the exercise that gives them the information they need and reassign the work. "Let's see who can get it this time . . . .")

(**Note:** A ✔ tells you to check what the students are doing. A check sometimes appears when students have to find something in their textbook. A check requires only a second or two. If you are positioned close to several "average performing" students, check whether they are performing. If they are, proceed with the presentation.)

ARROW 4: BOARD WORK

What you write is indicated in the display boxes of the script. In the sample exercise, you write the sentence as it is shown in the display. Scanning the display boxes shows both what you'll write and how you'll change the display.

Managing Writing Activities

The writing activities in each lesson work on specific skills. Most writing activities involve the following:

- an introduction
- student writing
- teacher reading of model passage
- student oral reading of some passages
- editing and revising passage

The two basic rules that you should follow throughout Level F are:

1) Structure the teaching so that students receive success at a high rate, and praise them for success;

2) When students orally read what they have written, don't overlook obvious mistakes of usage or of following the directions. Do not accept writing that is unacceptable (sentences that are not sentences, wording that does not follow the model, sentences that are vague). Point out mistakes. Direct students to correct mistakes.

Oral reading accounts for possibly half of what students learn about writing. Students learn both from the good models that are read and from the mistakes in the poor models. The oral reading of passages, therefore, is extremely important in shaping the students' understanding of how to apply what they have learned to specific writing assignments.

The program is designed so that all appropriately placed students should be able to write all assignments acceptably. If the student success rate is high, corrections will tend not to frustrate students, because the chances are great that they'll do it correctly next time and will receive your praise. Also, if they make a mistake, it is a mistake that should be corrected.

The most important reason for pointing out mistakes and for reinforcing students for identifying mistakes is that the passages read aloud serve as a model for other students. If you fail to respond to passages or sentences that have obvious problems, the other students will understandably assume that such writing is acceptable.

Effective management techniques for presenting writing assignments assure that students will learn from the models and will become facile at checking their own work. These techniques also reduce the amount of time you spend marking papers. (Following writing assignments, you mark papers.)

AS STUDENTS WRITE

Here are the basic rules to follow as students write:

1) **Direct students to write on every other line of their paper,** not on every line. This practice anticipates that students will need to make at least minor revisions and that such revisions can be achieved without extensive erasing and crowding if students have extra spaces for making corrections.

2) **Make a line in the margin to mark what you've already read.** Read passages as students are writing. If you become practiced at moving from student to student, you can read most of what students write as they are writing.

3) **Put a dot in the margin on any line that has a problem.** The student may try to find the problem, or you may tell the student what the problem is. Refer to the criteria given in the instructions when commenting on what students have written. If students did not follow the directions, tell them which directions they didn't follow. "You were supposed to tell how much more. I think some of your sentences have problems. Read over what you've written and see if you can fix it up." When you read the passage later, you can scan the part you've already read to see if the mistake has been corrected.

4) **Do not spend a lot of time with one student.** There will be time for fix-ups later. Don't stand around as a student tries to find and correct the problem. Instead, observe other students and possibly return to the student who had the problem later.

5) **Make frequent comments to the class as you read what students are writing.** These comments should focus on what students are doing well and specific mistakes observed in several students' writing. "Wow, we have some good specific directions."

   If students have had problems with a particular skill in the past and are doing well, make comments to the class. "You are doing a super job telling why the evidence is irrelevant."

6) **Do not wait for all students to complete an in-class assignment.** Allow a reasonable amount of time based on the performance of a student who performs at a reasonable rate. A minute or two before students are to stop writing, tell how much time is left. When you tell students to stop, they are to put their pencil down. *Note:* If you wait for all students to finish, students' writing rate will not improve greatly because there's no payoff for writing faster. If writing rate is a problem, reinforce students who complete assignments within a reasonable time period.

   Many exercises are multi-step activities in which the students write an extended passage part by part. Students who have not finished writing a part should put their pencil down and listen to the oral reading of that part. After the oral reading, you'll give directions for writing the next part. Students who do not finish the preceding part should leave space for finishing that part. They should begin work on the next part.

7) **Praise improvement.** Make announcements to the class as you observe students. Be sure to praise improvement of the low performers. "Well, you sure wrote a lot more today than you did last time. Good writing. Keep it up."

STUDENTS' ORAL READING OF SENTENCES AND PASSAGES

Following the writing, you will call on a few students to read what they've written. You will point out specific problems and engage the class in attending to mistakes as well as to aspects that are good. Here are the general rules to follow:

1) Call on a mix of higher- and lower-performing students. However, do not call on lower performers unless you know that what they've written has very few mistakes. (You've read the passage or most of it.)

2) Make sure that students attend to the passages that are orally read and identify specific problems. Direct students to raise their hand if they have a problem. A good technique is to model the behavior that you want students to perform. When you hear a problem, raise your hand. You may provide some kind of reinforcement for students who identify problems correctly.

3) Establish a general rule that students are not to make fun of another student's writing. Also let students know that mistakes are a part of writing and that fixing up mistakes is an important part of the writing process.

4) Make sure students receive specific information about how to revise any mistake.

5) When a student reads aloud, first determine whether the student followed the directions you gave. If not, say flatly something like, "That didn't follow the directions. You'll have to fix it up later."

Next, determine whether the sentences are appropriately worded. Appropriate wording is clear. If what the student wrote is clear and follows the directions, it is acceptable. Even if the student's sentence is not exactly the same as the model the script provides, the sentence may be perfectly acceptable. For some assignments, there is very little latitude in the sentences students write. As a rule, near the end of the program a much wider range of sentences is acceptable for expressing ideas.

Respond to specific wording problems. If something is phrased awkwardly or is vague, point out the problem. "That's right, but it could be worded more clearly." Either provide the alternative wording or call on another student for a suggestion.

6) Remind students that they are working on difficult material. Say things like, "Writing these sentences is very hard. Many adults would have trouble expressing these ideas." Within this context, mistakes are not symbols of failures.

REVISING AND EDITING
Before students hand in their paper they are to correct any problems by rewriting sentences, fixing up punctuation errors and putting in information that had been omitted.

1) Make revision a standard part of each assignment. If revising becomes routine, it is not a "punishment." It's something that everybody does. Follow the general rule: When you hand it in, it should be corrected and well written.

2) If possible, allow about 5 minutes at the end of each lesson for students to revise and edit their writing. They are to revise any wording that was unclear, add necessary words or sentences and make sure sentences are punctuated correctly.

3) For minor changes, direct students to cross out the word or part that is wrong, make a caret (∧) to indicate where the inserted material goes and write the corrected part on the line above the mistake or omission.

only one dollar
A new Bumpo costs 2 dollars less than last year's Bumpo.

If a student left out a sentence, the student may write the sentence at the top or bottom of the page and make an arrow to show where it should be inserted.

4) If extensive revision is needed to make the assignment acceptable, assign the fix-up as homework and tell students to rewrite the passage completely. "Make sure you know what changes you want to make. Rewrite the whole passage. Then read it to yourself and make sure it says what you want it to say." At least half the mistakes students make are sentences that do not say what students think they say.

5) Possibly you can establish a peer-checking procedure. Assign the upper one-third of the students to be "checkers." Their role is to read over corrected passages and identify any possible problems. The advantage of using peer checkers is that students receive more timely feedback.

MARKING PAPERS
After students revise and edit their work, they hand it in. You mark it. The line you marked in the margin indicates how much of each paper you've already checked. Any dots you marked in the margin indicate sentences that had problems. By scanning first to see if problem sentences were corrected and then reading the remainder of the paper, you should be able to process each paper quickly.

The comments you will write on the paper should help students learn and should reinforce good practices.

1) Correct improper grammar by writing the correct words above the incorrect ones. For instance, if a student writes, *The car did not have no guarantee,* cross out the word *no* and write *a* above it.

2) Do not penalize students for all spelling mistakes. A good rule is to hold the students accountable for any "spelling words" they should know and any words in the fact tables or instructions. You can write **S** or **Sp** above these words to indicate they are misspelled. Do not write the correct spelling. If you wish to show the student the spelling of **other misspelled words,** write the word above the misspelled word.

3) Make comments on the paper. You may use letter grades or just comments. Try to focus on improvement even if a paper has serious problems.

Much better. Watch run-ons.

For good papers, write comments such as:

Superior! or *Great job!*

4) Try to return students' papers before the next scheduled language lesson. Students are to fix up any mistakes before you begin the next lesson. They are to show you that they have fixed up the mistakes. A good practice is to tell the students to put their corrected papers on their desk at the beginning of the next language lesson. You can either check the fix-ups then, or you can do it as part of your observation when students write their passage for the current lesson.

GRADING PAPERS

Base the paper grading system on the number of uncorrected errors in the work the students hand in and on a careful grading of every third to fifth lesson.

Because of the amount of material that students write, it is difficult to grade papers every day. A good procedure is to check some parts each day.

- Check the **independent work** for each lesson. Read each student's work and mark errors.

- Also check the **parts of the class work** that require the students to compose sentences. The models for those parts are indicated in the teacher's *Presentation Book* with double lines (‖) in the margin. Make sure that the students' compositions a) follow the model and b) have sentences that are acceptable.

- Also check whether students completed the parts of the lesson. Give students credit for the parts by awarding one point per part and a bonus of two points for correcting all parts. (If the work consists of five parts, students who do all the parts and correct them would receive seven points.)

- Require students to redo any parts that are unacceptable. By requiring students to redo work, you provide them with an understanding of your standards.

- **Carefully grade every third to fifth lesson.** Don't tell students which lessons will be graded carefully. Grade all parts of the lesson, including the independent work. Award bonus points for each part that is perfect.

A reinforcement system may be needed to ensure that students put serious effort into writing assignments. The system should demonstrate clearly to students that there is a payoff for turning in excellent work. **Key the system to paper grading.**

USING THE ANSWER KEY

A separate *Answer Key* booklet for Level F provides guidelines for each part of all non-test lessons.

What students write appears in italics:

$$\overset{V}{\underline{Could}} \quad \overset{N}{\underline{\textcircled{Jimmy}}} \quad \overset{V}{\underline{help \ us?}}$$

3. *Could (Jimmy) help us?*

Instructions to you, the teacher, appear in regular type.

The *Answer Key* indicates specific wording or specific parts of wording that are not negotiable. The student's paper must include these words. The key also indicates where students have latitude in what they write. As a rule, the farther students go in the program, the less specific the answer-key specifications are because students have learned a variety of optional ways of creating acceptable sentences and paragraphs.

Parentheses ( ) around a word or group of words indicate that the part is optional. The student response is correct if this part does not appear.

Example:
Make an upside-down A (that is) one inch high.

The student's response is to be considered correct if the words **that is** do not appear.

Brackets [ ] around a word or group of words indicate that an answer can be considered correct if the student expresses the **idea** but not the **words** shown inside the brackets.

Example:
The square [is just under the middle of the line].

The student writes:
The square is just below the center of the line.

The student's response is perfectly acceptable—it clearly expresses the same idea as the words inside the brackets.

Either/or { / } indicates acceptable alternatives.

Example:
{Make/Write} a B on the left end of the line.

Sentences with the verb **make** or **write** are equally acceptable.

Tracks

This section describes the major tracks developed in Level F. Each track deals with a significant topic. Activities from each track appear in a large range of lessons. In a particular lesson, activities from more than one track are presented. (See the scope and sequence chart on pages 2 and 3.) Here is an outline of the major tracks:

Retell
Grammar and Usage
    Sentences
    Nouns
    Pronouns
    Adjectives
    Verbs
    Verb Tense Agreement
    Adverbs
    Using Adverbs and Adjectives Correctly
    Parallelism
    Possessives
    Subject-Verb Agreement
    Passive to Active
    Cumulative
General/Specific
    More-General—More-Specific
    Definitions
    Appositives
    Appropriate Category Words
Clarity of Meaning
    Comparatives
    Descriptions
    Essential and Nonessential Elements
    Ambiguous Adjectives
    Ambiguous Verbs
Deductions and Inferences
    Drawing Conclusions from Evidence
    Discrediting Rules
    Constructing Rules from Observations
    Consistency
Writing
    Critiquing
        Wrong Conclusions
    Invalid Arguments
        Other Possibilities
        Using Criteria to Make Decisions
        More-General Conclusions
    Ambiguous Meanings

Unclear Directions
Misleading Information
    Individual-Group Fallacies
    Part-Whole Fallacies
    Misleading Statistics
Comparing and Synthesizing Information
    Compare and Contrast
    Identifying Reliable Sources
    Synthesizing Information
    Similes
    Analogies
Rule Generating, Rule Testing, and Consistency
    Rule Testing
    Revising Rules Based on New Evidence
    Noting Inconsistencies and Contradictions
    Designing Experiments
    False Cause

Retell

The retell activities presented in Level F require students to (a) remember details of what is presented orally, (b) organize information around headings, such as who, when, where, details, and (c) reconstruct sentences that were said.

Retell activities are designed to strengthen the students' awareness of details. Students who are able to recall the details of what was said are more able to take notes that permit them to reconstruct the important details of the original passage. These students are also in a position to integrate models of good sentences into this repertoire. The work with retell begins in lesson 7.

Typically, students are initially poor at retelling. Their attempts to retell even simple passages frequently result in sentence fragments, serious omissions of detail and unclear sentences. The problem with the students' initial performance results at least partly from the fact that they may never have been required to pay careful attention to what is said and to reproduce the content.

Just as typically, however, students' performance improves dramatically after three or four retells. Note, however, that this often dramatic improvement in retell ability comes about only if the students understand what is expected and are held to a hard criterion of performance during the initial exercises.

The teacher first puts on the board the headings for notes the students will take. The teacher reads the entire passage, and then presents the passage a part at a time as students write each part. Finally, the teacher rereads the whole passage. Students mark each sentence that has the same meaning as the sentence the teacher dictated. Here's the introduction to retells from lesson 7:

1. (Write on the board:)

> **Who:**
> **When:**
> **Where:**
> **Details:**

2. You're going to see how many details of a report you can remember and write.
   * The headings on the board show the main points you'll attend to.
   * You'll indicate **who** did it.
   * You'll indicate **when** the person did it and **where.**
   * Then you'll indicate other key **details** of what the person did.

3. Write **R** on your paper. **R** stands for **retell.** ✔
   * Copy the headings: **who, when, where** and **details.**
   * Leave a space after each heading because you'll take notes for retelling the report.
   * Put your pencils down after you've written your headings. ✔

4. I'll read the report two times. After the first time I read it, you can write notes about who, when, where and other details.

   * During the second reading, you can fill in more details in your notes or just retell the report. Your goal is to write the report so it is as close as possible to the report I read.
   * Don't write anything until I've read the report one time.

5. Listen:

   At 6:22 a.m. on Saturday morning, the Human Fly climbed the Bank Tower Building. He went straight up the smooth glass wall of the 40-story building. His hands were bare and empty, but they seemed to stick to the wall. His feet were clad in ordinary sneakers. It took the Human Fly about 20 minutes to reach the top. Then he disappeared without a trace.

6. Write your notes—tell who, when, where and other details. Don't write sentences, just notes.
   (Observe students and give feedback.)

7. I'll read the report again. You can add to your notes as I read. Then you'll write it so it's very close to the report I read.
   * Listen:

   At 6:22 a.m. on Saturday morning, the Human Fly climbed the Bank Tower Building. He went straight up the smooth glass wall of the 40-story building. His hands were bare and empty, but they seemed to stick to the wall. His feet were clad in ordinary sneakers. It took the Human Fly about 20 minutes to reach the top. Then he disappeared without a trace.

8. Write your report. Pencils down when you're finished.
   (Observe students and give feedback.)

9. (Write on the board:)

> **Who:**   **Human Fly**
> **When:**   **6:22 a.m. Saturday**
> **Where:**   **Bank Tower Building**
> **Details:** **40 stories, 20 minutes, bare hands, sneakers, disappeared**

- Here are some good notes. They tell who, when and where.
- Look at the details. What does the 40 stories refer to? (Call on a student.) *The Bank Tower Building.*
- What does the 20 minutes refer to? (Call on a student.) *How long it took the Human Fly to reach the top of the building.*
- If you wrote notes like these, you could reproduce the important information from the original report.
- (Call on several students to read their notes. Point out: lack of important information; notes that are too long or that are in sentence form.)
10. (Call on several students to read their report. Praise reports that approximate the original. Praise sentences that are very close or identical to those in the original report.)

Teaching Notes

When you present the first reading of the retell:

1) Make sure that students do not write as you talk. Pencils are down.
2) Don't permit students to write until you tell them to write.
3) Permit students only a reasonable amount of time to write the sentences. Do not necessarily wait for the last person to finish.
4) Remember to move around the room as you present this exercise, and comment on students who are doing a good job. Say things like, "I see some sentences that are (very close/identical) to the sentences I said. I see people who are punctuating correctly."
5) When students write, convey the idea that the sentences do not have to be identical to the sentences you

dictated; however, they should be very close and should contain all the information you conveyed in your sentences. If sentences are lacking in detail, tell students, "You missed a lot of information."
6) Remind students that they will become a lot better at retell tasks. "This was our first retell exercise. It was hard, but you're going to do a lot of work with retell, and you'll get a lot better at it if you work hard and think about it."

In step 9, you check the students' notes. Often, students don't understand why they are taking notes. They don't appreciate that notes give them clues that permit them to reconstruct sentences. You can model the process by saying things like, "Here are good notes for details: **40 stories; 20 minutes; bare hands; sneakers; disappeared.** If I have those notes, I can write sentences because I know the main thing they'll say. What sentence would I write using the words **40 stories?**" Praise sentences like, **He went straight up a 40-story building.**

"Another note is **20 minutes. What sentence would I write for 20 minutes?**" Praise sentences such as, **The Human Fly got to the top of the building in 20 minutes.** Or, **It took the Human Fly 20 minutes to get to the top.** "If I don't take notes that give me specific information, I don't have the key information I need. What if my note just says, **tall building?** Now I may not be able to write the sentence about the building being 40 stories tall because my notes don't help me out." Tell students with poor notes to include the details that are in your sample notes.

Criteria for acceptable work:

1) **Spelling.** A general rule is that students are held accountable for the correct spelling of any word on their spelling lists and for words that appear in the textbook.

2) **Fidelity of retell passages.** Did the student write a sentence for every idea in the original passage? Is the sentence actually a sentence and not simply a group of words? Is the sentence punctuated properly, at least to the extent that it begins with a capital and ends with a period? Does the sentence express the same central idea as the original?

The same criteria apply throughout the retell track. Sentences must express the ideas of the originals. Although students may amalgamate sentences (especially when they retell longer passages), the key information must be retained in their passages.

In later lessons, the retell exercises change. Starting with lesson 37, students write about more difficult topics. Here's the presentation from lesson 37.

Part D

Mona Lisa

Vocabulary Box · Leonardo da Vinci · Italy · Paris · detectives · France

1. (Write on the board:)

Who:
When:
Where:
Details:

2. Find part D.
• (Teacher reference:)

• This is a copy of a famous picture called the Mona Lisa. You're going to retell a passage about the Mona Lisa.

3. In your retell, you're going to tell about **what,** not **who.**
• You'll have a lot of information for **when.** You'll have some information for **where** and **details.**

4. Write part **R** on your paper. Copy the headings. Make sure you have a lot of space after **when.** Pencils down when you're ready. ✔

5. I'll read the passage two times. You'll take notes after the first reading.
• When you listen to the passage, think about **what, when, where** and **the details** that are described.

6. Some of the names that you'll use in your notes are written in part D.
• The names are: **Mona Lisa, Leonardo da Vinci, Italy, Paris, detectives, France.**

7. Listen to the passage:
    The Mona Lisa is one of the most famous paintings in the world. It pictures an Italian woman. It was painted around 1500 by Leonardo da Vinci. For three hundred years, it hung in a museum in Paris, France. But in 1911, the museum reported that the Mona Lisa was missing. For two years, detectives were unable to find a single clue. Finally, in 1913, the painting was found in Italy. An Italian worker had stolen it. He said that the Mona Lisa should remain in Italy because it was painted in Italy. In 1914, the Mona Lisa was returned to France.

8. Write your notes. Pencils down when you're finished.
   (Observe students and give feedback.)
9. I'll read the passage one more time. You can take more notes if you want to. Then you'll write the passage.
   - Listen:
     The Mona Lisa is one of the most famous paintings in the world. It pictures an Italian woman. It was painted around 1500 by Leonardo da Vinci. For three hundred years, it hung in a museum in Paris, France. But in 1911, the museum reported that the Mona Lisa was missing. For two years, detectives were unable to find a single clue. Finally, in 1913, the painting was found in Italy. An Italian worker had stolen it. He said that the Mona Lisa should remain in Italy because it was painted in Italy. In 1914, the Mona Lisa was returned to France.
10. Rewrite the passage. Pencils down when you're finished.
    (Observe students and give feedback.)
11. (Write on the board:)

What:	**Mona Lisa—painted by Leonardo da Vinci**
When:	**1500;**
	stolen in 1911;
	found 1913;
	returned to France—1914
Where:	**300 years in France;**
	Italy;
	France
Details:	**stolen by worker;**
	should be in Italy

   - Here are some good notes.
   - (Call on several students to read their notes. Point out: lack of important information; notes that are too long or in sentence form; good entries.)
12. (Call on several students to read their passage. Praise accounts that approximate the original. Praise sentences that are very close or identical to those in the original passage.)

Teaching Notes

In step 6, you refer students to the vocabulary box. Students use the box in step 10 after they write their passage. They first write their passage without concerning themselves too much about spelling. The reason for this is that, if they try to attend to both the content and the spelling of words, they will write far less fluently and rapidly than they would if they simply wrote the words.

This format applies to the full range of writing topics: First put down your ideas; then edit. When you observe and give students feedback, make sure that they are attending to the spelling of the words in the vocabulary box and that they are checking to make sure that their sentences are sentences. If students are not attending to spelling, introduce a contingency for fixing up the spelling of all words that are in the vocabulary box—"Two extra points for the correct spelling of all the vocabulary words."

Students are not permitted to take notes during the first reading of the passage. They are permitted to take notes during the second reading; however, point out that you can read each paragraph only one more time. If students have trouble with the passage (producing poor retell passages) repeat the exercise during the following lesson. Tell students, "Listen very carefully and try to write notes that will let you write a passage very close to what I say." Don't be shy about telling the students, "This is very difficult work." It is.

ADDITIONAL RETELL ACTIVITIES

You are encouraged to present retell passages other than those specified in the lessons. The skills that students acquire through retell exercises make it possible for them to retell a variety of information passages. For example, as a part of social studies, you may want to present a retell passage on a topic under discussion. You may also want students to look up information and report it to the group. An excellent activity is for the reporting student to read the report twice (given that the report is not more than 100 words). During the first reading, the other students listen. During the second reading, they take notes for each main part. Then they reconstruct the passage. If the passage involves key words that the student doesn't know how to spell, write the words on the board.

Note that these activities are simple extensions of what occurs in Level F. If students perform well on the later passages in Level F, they have the organizational and writing skills necessary to perform well on these additional passages.

Grammar and Usage

Level F reviews complete sentences, nouns, verbs and pronouns (which are taught in earlier levels). Level F introduces work with adverbs and conjunctions. Level F also presents exercises involving possessives, subject-verb agreement and the correct use of adverbs or adjectives. Exercises introduce verbs of the senses and the rules for using adjectives with these verbs.

The first 14 lessons review sentences, nouns, verbs, pronouns and adjectives. Students learn tests for different parts of speech.

SENTENCES

In lesson 1, students discriminate between sentences and fragments. The context is a conversation. The students indicate whether the various remarks that Fran makes are sentences. Here's the conversation.

---

1. Don: Where did you go yesterday afternoon?
   Fran: To the fair.
2. Don: You said that you were going to go to the mall with me, but you didn't even call me.
   Fran: Sorry about that.
3. Fran: It slipped my mind.
4. Don: That makes me mad. You weren't very considerate.
   Fran: You are right.
5. Don: Who went to the fair with you?
   Fran: Mike.
6. Don: Well, why didn't you invite me to go along with you?
   Fran: I told you that I forgot.
7. Don: You really like Mike better than me, don't you?
   Fran: That is not true.
8. Don: Well, we could go some place next Saturday. Where would you like to go?
   Fran: The mall.

Note that students are often confused about sentences. Some of their more serious misconceptions are:

1. If it's a sentence, it has a lot of words. (Students would reject the idea that **She walked** is a sentence.)
2. If it expresses a complete thought, it is a sentence. (In a conversation, much of what Fran says is a complete thought but is not a sentence.)
3. If it has a capital and a period, it's a sentence.
4. If it's a sentence, it has commas and other marks to decorate it.

The thrust in Level F is to teach students to use sentences that are functional. Those are sentences that are not needlessly complicated to convey the information that must be conveyed to the reader. Students are not encouraged to write elaborate sentences or sentences that begin with a part other than the subject.

Although Level F does not get into a specific analysis of sentences, the basic sentence is in the order of subject-predicate. The subject names something; the predicate tells more about what is named. Sentences of this form usually require no punctuation other than a period. If part of the predicate is moved, punctuation is required:

He went to the store in the afternoon.
In the afternoon, he went to the store.

Punctuation is also required if words are missing:

He stood and watched and listened.
He stood, watched and listened.

Punctuation is required if unneeded parts are added to the sentence. Here's a sentence that has a part that is not needed to convey the necessary information: Our neighbors, **who live in the white house across the street,** have many friends. Whether or not the underlined part is to be set off by commas depends on whether the underlined part gives information needed to identify the neighbors. If not needed, the part is set off with commas.

If students are confused about sentences, repeat the sentence exercises that occur early in Level F (both the structured activity in lesson 1 and the independent work that appears in lessons 2, 4 and 6). Make sure that students can both identify fragments and make them into sentences that are appropriate for the context in which the fragment occurs.

NOUNS

In lesson 1, students apply this test for nouns: If the word names something when you put the word **one** or **some** in front of it, the word is a noun. Here are the words that students test:

1. quickly	7. always
2. beautiful	8. events
3. argument	9. noise
4. water	10. north
5. seeds	11. old
6. hungry	12. sister

Note that words like **water** and **noise** require the word **some.** Words like **argument** and **sister** require **one.**

PRONOUNS

In lesson 5, students replace the ending adjective and noun with an appropriate pronoun. Here is part of the exercise from lesson 5.

Part B | The last two words in each sentence are an adjective and a noun. Replace that part with a pronoun that makes sense.

1. John walked with his cane.
2. The engine of the train pulled 15 cars.
3. Don had an argument with his sister.
4. Frank drank cold water.
5. Mr. Jackson fixed large hamburgers.
6. Mrs. Taylor was proud of her son.

---

2. Find part B.
 • The last two words in each sentence are an adjective and a noun. You'll replace that part with a pronoun that makes sense.
3. Item 1: **John walked with his cane.**
 • What are the last two words? (Signal.) *His cane.*
4. Write the pronoun that replaces **his cane.** Then write the correct pronoun for the rest of the items in part B. Pencils down when you're finished. **(Observe students and give feedback.)**
5. Check your work.
 • Item 1: **John walked with his cane.** What pronoun replaces **his cane?** (Signal.) *It.*
 • Item 2: **The engine of the train pulled 15 cars.** What pronoun replaces **15 cars?** (Signal.) *Them.*
 • Item 3: **Don had an argument with his sister.** What pronoun replaces **his sister?** (Signal.) *Her.*
 • Item 4: **Frank drank cold water.** What pronoun replaces **cold water?** (Signal.) *It.*
 • Item 5: **Mr. Jackson fixed large hamburgers.** What pronoun replaces **large hamburgers?** (Signal.) *Them.*
 • Item 6: **Mrs. Taylor was proud of her son.** What pronoun replaces **her son?** (Signal.) *Him.*

Teaching Notes

In step 4, you observe and give feedback. Follow these rules:

1. Don't provide individual tutoring. If students have questions, tell them what they're supposed to do: "Write the pronoun that replaces the words **his cane.** The pronoun could be **he, she, it, they, them.** Pick the right word and write it." Remember, you will be showing students the correct answer in a moment.

2. Do not wait for all students to finish. It should take the students about 10 seconds to write the correct answer. Allow about 10 seconds—not 2 minutes. Then proceed with step 5.

3. If students make a large number of mistakes on this part, or if they do not follow your directions, repeat the part. After they have completed it, say, "That was pretty good. Now that you know the correct answers, let's do that exercise again, the right way. Turn your paper over so you can't see the correct answers . . . ." Repeat the exercise from step 2. Use this same practice for other skills early in the program. Remember, the set of items is often sufficient to teach students the discriminations. If they do poorly on a part (e.g., Part B) however, they will not learn the discrimination. Therefore, repeat the part. If it's not convenient to repeat the part now, tell the students you'll repeat it during the next lesson.

4. Make sure that students correct their papers when you give the correct answers.

Note that the adjectives include **his** and **her.** The students may have serious misconceptions about parts of speech and may think that **his** and **her** are always

pronouns. In these sentences, they are adjectives because they come before the noun and tell about the noun. They tell what kind.

ADJECTIVES

In lesson 8, students are provided with a test for adjectives: If the word tells what kind or how many, it's an adjective. Students work with sentences that end in adjectives. They rewrite the ending so the last word is an appropriate noun. Here's part of the exercise from lesson 8.

Part C   Use two or three words to rewrite the ending of each sentence so it ends with a noun. Then label the parts of speech for the new ending of the sentence.

1. His daughter was lovely.
2. The dictionary is useful.
3. Cabbage is nutritious.
4. A hurricane is powerful.
5. Jets are fast.

---

2. Find part C.
  * Each sentence ends with an adjective. You'll write two or three words that show the adjective with a noun.
3. Sentence 1: **His daughter was lovely.**
  * The last word is an adjective. You're going to rewrite the ending of the sentence so it ends with a noun.
  * Write three words: **His daughter was a lovely [something].** Write: **a lovely [something].** Pencils down when you're finished.
  (Observe students and give feedback.)
  * (Write on the board:)

  **a lovely person
  a lovely girl
  a lovely youngster**

  * Here are some possibilities: **a lovely person; a lovely girl; a lovely youngster.**
  * (Call on several students to read what they wrote.)
4. Listen: Write letters for the parts of speech. ✔

- The word **a** is an adjective. The word **lovely** is an adjective. The last word is a noun.
5. Sentence 2: **The dictionary is useful.**
- Write three words that show the adjectives and noun. Write letters above each word. Pencils down when you're finished.

    (Observe students and give feedback.)
- Here are some good endings: **a useful tool; a useful book; a useful resource.**
- The words **a** and **useful** are adjectives.
- (Call on several students to read what they wrote.)
6. Your turn: Write two or three words for the rest of the items in part C. Label the parts of speech for each word. Pencils down when you're finished.

    (Observe students and give feedback.)
7. Check your work.
- Sentence 3: **Cabbage is nutritious.** Here's a good ending: **a nutritious vegetable.**
- (Call on several students to read what they wrote.)
- Sentence 4: **A hurricane is powerful.** Here are some good endings: **a powerful storm; a powerful wind; powerful weather.**
- (Call on several students to read what they wrote.)
- Sentence 5: **Jets are fast.** Here are some good endings: **fast planes; fast vehicles.**
- (Call on several students to read what they wrote.)

Teaching Notes

In step 3, you provide Information about what to write for the first sentence. **Write three words: a lovely [something].** Do not go into elaborate discussions about what the students are to write. The more you explain, the longer it will be before some students

catch on to what they're supposed to do. The simplest procedure is to recognize that when students see the possible answers to the first item, they'll catch on and do well on the following items. Therefore, your goal should be to give them information about the first item as quickly as you can. Allow about 15 seconds for the students to write their responses. Give positive feedback to students who are writing acceptable endings. Then write the possibilities on the board. After you do, call on different students to read what they wrote. Praise acceptable answers, which would include: **a lovely individual; a lovely child; and a lovely daughter.** If students do repeat the word **daughter,** tell them that their answer is correct, "But you should be able to write another noun for that ending." If students have trouble generating good possibilities, repeat the exercise.

VERBS

The tests for verbs are introduced in lesson 12. The part of the sentence that is a verb tells whether there is one or more than one actor. The verb also tells whether the sentence refers to the past, the present or the future. Here's part of the exercise from lesson 12.

	Actor(s)	Verb	Other words
1.	■	looks	■ .
2.	■	were riding	■ .
3.	■	will go	■ .
4.	■	is wondering	■ .
5.	■	bought	■ .
6.	■	see	■ .
7.	■	stops	■ .

4. Sentence 1. The verb is: **looks.**
- Write the letter **X, Y** or **Z** to tell about the verb. **X** is for one actor; **Y** is for more than one actor; **Z** is for one actor **or** more than one actor.
- Pencils down when you've written the letter for sentence 1. ✔
- Everybody, what letter did you write? (Signal.) *X.*
- The verb tells about one actor. You could say: **She** looks at the dog. It's not correct to say: **They** looks at the dog.

5. Sentence 2. The verb is: **were riding.**
- Say sentences to yourself. Say one that starts with **She were riding** and a parallel sentence that starts with **They were riding.**
- Then write the letter that tells about the verb in sentence 2. Pencils down when you're finished.

  (Observe students and give feedback.)
- You should have written **Y.** The verb tells about more than one actor. You could say: **They** were riding horses. It's not correct to say: **She** were riding horses.

Teaching Notes

Make sure that students are firm. For some students, this work will be quite easy. For others, it may be more difficult than you would imagine. Make sure that those students can generate the sentences that start with pronouns. This exercise is repeated in several later lessons.

By lesson 16, students indicate whether the sentence refers to one actor or more than one; they indicate whether the sentence refers to the past, present or future; and they write a sentence that begins with an appropriate pronoun. Here's the exercise from lesson 16.

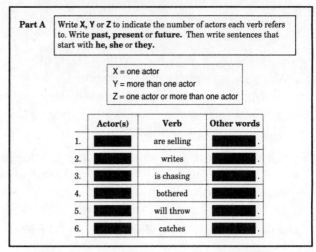

1. Open your book to lesson 16 and find part A. ✔
- These are sentences with only the verb shown.
- You're going to do three things for each item. You'll first indicate **X, Y** or **Z** to tell about the number of actors the verb refers to. Second, you'll tell about the time period. You'll write **past, present** or **future.** Third, you'll write sentences that start with **he, she** or **they** and that use the verb that is shown. If the verb tells about either one or more than one, you'll write **Z.** Write two parallel sentences for verbs you marked **Z.**
2. Item 1. The verb is: **are selling**
- Write **X, Y** or **Z** to show whether that verb refers to one actor or more than one actor. Pencils down when you're finished. ✔
- Everybody, what did you write? (Signal.) *Y.*
- Now write **past, present** or **future** to tell about the time period. Pencils down when you're finished. ✔
- Everybody, what did you write? (Signal.) *Present.*
- Now write a sentence that uses **he, she** or **they** and the verb. Pencils down when you're finished.

  (Observe students and give feedback.)
- Read your sentence for item 1. (Call on several students. Praise sentences of the form: **They are selling _____.)**

3. Your turn: Write **X, Y** or **Z** and **past, present** or **future** and a sentence for item 2. Pencils down when you're finished.
   (Observe students and give feedback.)
   - The verb for item 2 is: **writes.**
   - You should have written: **X.** That verb tells about one actor. You should have written: **present.** And your sentence should say something like: **He writes poor paragraphs.**
   - Read your sentence for item 2. (Call on several students to read their sentence. Praise sentences of the form: **{He/She} writes _____.**)
4. Your turn: Do the rest of the items in part A. Pencils down when you're finished.
   (Observe students and give feedback.)
5. Find the key at the back of your book on page 311. ✔
   - That shows whether you should have for **X, Y** or **Z** and the time periods for all the items in part A.
6. Read your sentence for item 3. (Call on different students to read their sentence. Repeat step 6 with items 4 through 6.)

   Key:
   1. Y
      present
      They are selling _____.
   2. X
      present
      {He/She} writes _____.
   3. X
      present
      {He/She} is chasing _____.
   4. Z
      past
      {He/She} bothered _____.
      They bothered _____.
   5. Z
      future
      {He/She} will throw _____.
      They will throw _____.
   6. X
      present
      {He/She} catches_____.

In lesson 17, students discriminate between verbs and non-verbs. They use the test that if the words are verbs, they tell both about the number of actors and the time when the action took place.

VERB-TENSE AGREEMENT

In lesson 24, students learn the rule that if a sentence refers to something that is always true, the sentence uses a present tense verb. **"Birds fly"** is something that is always true.

In lesson 26, students begin editing passages that have inconsistent verb tenses. Here's the passage from lesson 26.

> **Passage**
>
> Linda and Andrew almost had a serious accident. They were crossing a small stream. A support on the bridge broke. Suddenly, the bridge tilts to one side. Andrew almost falls off. He grabs Linda. Then she almost slid off the bridge with him. Finally, Andrew grabbed a rail. He hung onto it, and Linda climbed over him. She got off the bridge first.
>
> In the meantime, Andrew is losing his grip on the rail. A young man came by and saw what happened. He crawled out to where Andrew was and helped Andrew get off the bridge.

Students identify the four sentences that have the wrong tense and rewrite those sentences in the past tense.

ADVERBS

In lesson 31, students are introduced to adverbs. The test is whether the word tells where, when or how. Students use this test to determine whether the last word in a sentence is a noun or an adverb. Here's the student exercise from lesson 31.

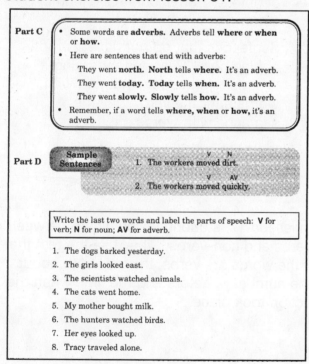

Part C
- Some words are **adverbs**. Adverbs tell **where** or **when** or **how**.
- Here are sentences that end with adverbs:
    They went **north**. **North** tells **where**. It's an adverb.
    They went **today**. **Today** tells **when**. It's an adverb.
    They went **slowly**. **Slowly** tells **how**. It's an adverb.
- Remember, if a word tells **where, when** or **how**, it's an adverb.

Part D **Sample Sentences**

    1. The workers moved dirt.
    2. The workers moved quickly.

Write the last two words and label the parts of speech: **V** for verb; **N** for noun; **AV** for adverb.

1. The dogs barked yesterday.
2. The girls looked east.
3. The scientists watched animals.
4. The cats went home.
5. My mother bought milk.
6. The hunters watched birds.
7. Her eyes looked up.
8. Tracy traveled alone.

Students write the last two words and label them with the letters **V, N** or **AV**.

Teaching Notes

If students make mistakes with the last word, direct them to test the word: "Does the word tell about when, where, or how?" If the answer is yes: "Which one does it tell about?" If the answer is no: "Does the last word name a person, place or thing?" (Would the word make sense with the word **one** or **some** in front of it?)

In lesson 33, students discriminate between sentences that end with adjectives and those that end with adverbs. The test involves putting the last word of the sentence in front of the noun in the subject (the actor). If the two words make sense, the word being tested is an adjective. Here's part of the exercise from lesson 33.

3. Sentence 1: **The picture looked interesting.**
- Everybody, what's the noun in the subject? (Signal.) *Picture.*
- So you write **picture** with the word **interesting** in front of it. If the two words tell about the subject, the word **interesting** is an adjective.
- Write the two words and indicate the part of speech for each word. Pencils down when you're finished. (Observe students and give feedback.)
- (Write on the board:)

         A   N
1. interesting picture

- Here's what you should have written: **interesting picture.** That makes sense. So **interesting** is an adjective. **Picture** is a noun. Pencils down if you got it right.

4. Sentence 2: **The birds looked around.**
- Write the noun in the subject with the word **around** in front of it. Indicate the parts of speech. Pencils down when you're finished.
(Observe students and give feedback.)
- (Write on the board:)

> AV   N
> 2. around birds

- Here's what you should have written: **around birds.** That doesn't tell about the subject. So **around** is not an adjective. It's an adverb. It tells **where.** The word **birds** is a noun.
5. Your turn: Do the rest of the items in part F. Write the last word of the sentence in front of the noun in the subject. Indicate the parts of speech. Pencils down when you're finished.
(Observe students and give feedback.)
6. Find the key at the back of your book on page 313. ✔
- That shows what you should have for each item.
- Raise your hand if you got everything right.

Key:
```
         A         N
1. interesting picture
        AV    N
2. around birds
         A      N
3. beautiful birds
        A       N
4. difficult work
        A         N
5. longer shadows
       AV   N
6. down sun
       AV    N
7. here children
            A             N
8. complicated sentences
          AV     N
9. together birds
           A     N
10. tired workers
```

Teaching Notes

The teacher wording in the exercise refers to the noun in the subject. If students have trouble identifying the noun in the subject, tell them, "That's the actor in this sentence."

Note that the words that are adverbs include far more than words that end with **L–Y.**

USING ADVERBS AND ADJECTIVES CORRECTLY

In lesson 41, students determine whether verbs are **is verbs.** Those are forms of the verb **to be: is, was, am,** etc.

In lesson 42, students complete sentence pairs with the correct adverb or adjective form.

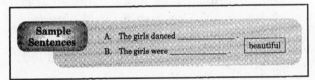

Sample Sentences
A. The girls danced _____
B. The girls were _____   beautiful

The word in the box is the adjective. It is appropriate for the sentence with the **is verb.** The adverb that is related to **beautiful** is **beautifully.** The adverb goes in the sentence that does not have an **is verb:**

> **The girls danced beautifully.**
> **The girls were beautiful.**

Here's part of the exercise from lesson 42.

Complete each sentence with the correct adjective or adverb.

1. a. He was talking _____ .
   b. He was _____ .   loud

2. a. The bug was _____ .
   b. The bug moved _____ .   slow

3. a. They walk _____ .
   b. They are _____ .   quick

4. a. Our friend dresses _____ .
   b. Our friend is _____ .   careful

5. a. He is _____ .
   b. He is driving _____ .   careless

4. Look at pair 1. The word in the box is **loud.** That's an adjective. What's the adverb? (Signal.) *Loudly.*

- Write the letters **A** and **B** for item 1. After **A,** write the word that completes sentence A. After **B,** write the word that completes sentence B. Pencils down when you've written the words for both sentences in item 1.
(Observe students and give feedback.)

- Check your work. Sentence A should say: **He was talking** *loudly.* Sentence B should say: **He was** *loud.*

5. Item 2. The word in the box is **slow.** That's an adjective. What's the adverb? (Signal.) *Slowly.*

- Write the word that completes each sentence in item 2. Pencils down when you're finished.
(Observe students and give feedback.)

- Check your work. Sentence A should say: **The bug was** *slow.* Sentence B should say: **The bug moved** *slowly.*

6. Item 3. The word in the box is **quick.** That's an adjective. What's the adverb? (Signal.) *Quickly.*

- Write the word that completes each sentence in item 3. Then do items 4 and 5. Pencils down when you're finished.
(Observe students and give feedback.)

7. Check your work.

- Item 3. Sentence A should say: **They walk** *quickly.* Sentence B should say: **They are** *quick.*

- Item 4. Sentence A should say: **Our friend dresses** *carefully.* Sentence B should say: **Our friend is** *careful.*

- Item 5. Sentence A should say: **He is** *careless.* Sentence B should say: **He is driving** *carelessly.*

8. Raise your hand if you got everything right. Everybody else, fix up any mistakes you made in part E.

Teaching Notes

This exercise assumes that students have a thorough understanding of **is verbs (am, is, are, was** and **were).** Verbs such as **is driving** (item 5) are not **is verbs.**

Students may make mistakes such as **He was talking loud** because that's what they hear. Tell them, "For proper writing, that's not correct, but sometimes people would say that sentence."

Students work on exercises similar to that in lesson 42 for six lessons.

In lesson 53, students learn that verbs of the senses take adjectives, not adverbs. Students work with sentences that end in an adjective. Some of the sentences are correct; some are incorrect. Students test the sentences by first identifying whether the verb is a verb of the senses. Those are verbs that tell how something feels, looks, smells, sounds or tastes. Here's part of the exercise from lesson 53.

Part D	All these sentences end in an adjective. Write **S** if the verb is a verb of the senses or **X** if it is not. Rewrite each sentence that you mark with an **X** so it ends with an adverb.

1. Those roses smell fragrant.
2. The dog barked loud.
3. The dog sounded loud.
4. Her coat felt rough.
5. Her coat protected thorough.
6. Her coat looked smooth.
7. She spoke smooth.
8. Her words sounded smooth.
9. She ran smooth.

2. Find part D.

- All these sentences end in an adjective. All these sentences have a verb that is not an **is** verb. If the verb is a **verb of the senses,** the adjective is correct. If the verb is **not** a verb of the senses, the adjective is wrong.

3. Copy the number of each sentence. Write **S** if the sentence is correct or **X** if it is wrong. The **S** means that the verb is a verb of the senses. Pencils down when you're finished.
(Observe students and give feedback.)

4. Check your work.

- Sentence 1: **Those roses smell fragrant.** Does the sentence use a verb of the senses? (Signal.) *Yes.*
- The sentence is correct so you should have marked **S** for sentence 1.
- Sentence 2: **The dog barked loud.** Does the sentence use a verb of the senses? (Signal.) *No.*
- Is the sentence correct? (Signal.) *No.*
- You should have marked **X** for sentence 2.
- Sentence 3: **The dog sounded loud.** Does the sentence use a verb of the senses? (Signal.) *Yes.*
- Is the sentence correct? (Signal.) *Yes.*
- You should have marked **S** for sentence 3.
- Sentence 4: **Her coat felt rough.** Does the sentence use a verb of the senses? (Signal.) *Yes.*
- Is the sentence correct? (Signal.) *Yes.*
- You should have marked **S** for sentence 4.
- Sentence 5: **Her coat protected thorough.** Does the sentence use a verb of the senses? (Signal.) *No.*
- Is the sentence correct? (Signal.) *No.*
- You should have marked **X** for sentence 5.
- Sentence 6: **Her coat looked smooth.** Does the sentence use a verb of the senses? (Signal.) *Yes.*
- Is the sentence correct? (Signal.) *Yes.*
- You should have marked **S** for sentence 6.
- Sentence 7: **She spoke smooth.** Does the sentence use a verb of the senses? (Signal.) *No.*
- Is the sentence correct? (Signal.) *No.*
- You should have marked **X** for sentence 7.
- Sentence 8: **Her words sounded smooth.** Does the sentence use a verb of the senses? (Signal.) *Yes.*
- Is the sentence correct? (Signal.) *Yes.*
- You should have marked **S** for sentence 8.

- Sentence 9: **She ran smooth.** Does the sentence use a verb of the senses? (Signal.) *No.*
- Is the sentence correct? (Signal.) *No.*
- You should have marked **X** for sentence 9.

5. Remember, if the verb tells how you **sensed** something, the adjective is correct.

6. Sentences **2, 5, 7** and **9** are wrong because they do not have an **is** verb or a **verb of the senses.**
- Rewrite each incorrect sentence so it ends with an adverb, not an adjective. Pencils down when you're finished.

(Observe students and give feedback.)

7. Find the key at the back of your book on page 315. ✔
- That shows what you should have for each sentence.

8. Sentence 2: The dog barked loudly.
- Sentence 5: Her coat protected thoroughly.
- Sentence 7: She spoke smoothly.
- Sentence 9: She ran smoothly.
- All these sentences have action verbs that are not verbs of the senses.

Teaching Notes

In step 3, students write **S** if the sentence shown is correct and **X** if it is wrong. If students make mistakes, ask, "What's the verb in the sentence? Is that a verb of the senses?" If students identify the verb but make a mistake about whether it is a verb of the senses, ask: "Does the verb _____ tell about feeling, looking, smelling, sounding or tasting?" If students do not respond correctly: "Which one does it tell about?" You test words by referring to the criteria introduced in the lesson to show how they are to use these tests. This information is very important.

PARALLELISM

Level F presents various activities that involve parallelism. Students make two sentences more parallel by increasing the number of words that are common to both sentences. The analysis of grammar is based on parallelism. If two words have the same function in the sentence, they are parallel. This means that you could substitute one word for the other, and the new word would both occupy the same position in the sentence and have the same role (telling number and tense, naming the actor, identifying how or when the actor performed, replacing a noun).

In lesson 48, students change model sentences so they are increasingly parallel. Here's part of the work from lesson 48.

Part B   For each sentence, write two sentences that are more parallel than the sentence shown.

1. That bird sings at sunrise and sunset.
2. We can use dirt from the hill or the river.
3. We will build the house in March or April.
4. Water leaks from the ceiling and the window.

---

2. Find part B.
- For each sentence, you're going to write two sentences that are more parallel than the sentence shown. The first variation of the sentence will be a little more parallel than the original. The second variation will be even more parallel.

3. Sentence 1: **That bird sings at sunrise and at sunset.**
- Write a sentence that is a little more parallel. Then write a second sentence that is even more parallel. Pencils down when you're finished.

  (Observe students and give feedback.)

- Here are some sentences you could have written:
  That bird sings at sunrise and **at** sunset. That bird sings at sunrise and **sings at** sunset. That bird sings at sunrise, and **that bird sings at** sunset.
- If you wrote the last sentence, you need a comma before the word **and.**

- (Call on several students to read their pair of sentences.)

4. Sentence 2: **We can use dirt from the hill or the river.**
- Write two sentences that are more parallel than sentence 2. Pencils down when you're finished.

  (Observe students and give feedback.)

- Here are some of the sentences you could have:
  We can use dirt from the hill or **from** the river.
  We can use dirt from the hill or **dirt from** the river.
  We can use dirt from the hill, or **we can use dirt from** the river.
  That last sentence needs a comma.

- (Call on several students to read their pair of sentences for item 2.)

5. Your turn: Write two parallel sentences for item 3 and for item 4. Pencils down when you're finished.

  (Observe students and give feedback.)

6. Find the key at the back of your book on page 315. ✔
- That shows the sentences you could have for items 3 and 4.
- Notice that only the last sentence for each item needs a comma. That's because the last sentence is the only one that is actually two complete sentences stuck together with the word **and** or **or.**

If students have trouble generating variations of parallel parts, write the original sentence on the board: **We can use dirt from the hill or the river.** Underline the words **the hill.**

"The part that is repeated in this sentence is parallel to **the hill.** What does that part say?" (Signal.) *The river.*

(Underline: **from the hill.**)

"What part is underlined now?" (Signal.) *From the hill.*

"What part is parallel to **from the hill?**" (Signal.) *From the river.*

(Underline: **dirt from the hill.**)

"What part is underlined now?" (Signal.) *Dirt from the hill.*

"What part is parallel to **dirt from the hill?**" (Signal.) *Dirt from the river.*

(Underline: **can use dirt from the hill.**)

"What part is underlined now?" (Signal.) *Can use dirt from the hill.*

"What part is parallel to **can use dirt from the hill?**" (Signal.) *Can use dirt from the river.*

POSSESSIVES

In lesson 52, students start work with the main noun of the subject. The main noun occurs in sentences that have more than one noun, such as: **The noise of the trains.** The main noun is **noise.** The verb must agree in number with the main noun. Students often have trouble identifying the main noun.

In Level F, the main-noun difficulties are partly solved by introducing a transformation. First, students work with sentences that have only one noun but that have a possessive adjective: **The train's noise . . . loud.** The only noun is **noise.** It refers to one, so the verb refers to one: **The train's noise was**

loud. In lesson 52, students indicate the correct verb for sentences of this type. Here's the exercise from the student's textbook.

Part B	For each item, write **is** or **are.**
	1. The tractors' wheels _____ red.
	2. The student's pens _____ expensive.
	3. The manager's argument _____ ridiculous.
	4. The Smith Building's doors _____ unlocked.
	5. The building's windows _____ dirty.
	6. The children's dog _____ sick.
	7. Our mother's cupcakes _____ delicious.
	8. Sally's horses _____ fast.

In lesson 53, students work with similar sentences. However, they rewrite them with two nouns. For **the campers' spirit,** they write, **the spirit of the campers.** The main noun is the same for both versions—**spirit.** Here's part of the exercise from lesson 53.

Rewrite each sentence so it has the word **of** and uses the correct verb, **was** or **were.**

1. The campers' spirit _____ high.
2. The door's sides _____ worn.
3. The trains' noise _____ loud.
4. The train's noises _____ irritating.
5. The smokestacks' odor _____ terrible.

3. Sentence 1. Raise your hand when you know the correct verb for the sentence the way it is written. ✔
   • What's the correct verb? (Signal.) *Was.*
   • That's the same verb the sentence will have when it is rewritten.
   • Rewrite sentence 1 so it has the word **of** and the verb **was.** Pencils down when you're finished.
   (Observe students and give feedback.)
   • Here's the sentence you should have written:
   ‖ The spirit **of** the campers **was** high.
   • Raise your hand if you got it right.
4. Rewrite sentence 2. Pencils down when you're finished.
   (Observe students and give feedback.)
   • Here's what you should have:
   The sides **of** the door **were** worn.
5. Rewrite sentence 3. Pencils down when you're finished.
   (Observe students and give feedback.)

- Here's what you should have:
  The noise **of** the trains **was** loud.
6. Remember, the same verb you have before you rewrite the sentence is the verb you use when you rewrite the sentence.
7. Your turn: Rewrite the rest of the sentences in part A. Pencils down when you're finished.

   (Observe students and give feedback.)
8. Find the key at the back of your book on page 315. ✔
- That shows what you should have for sentences 4 and 5.
- Raise your hand if you got everything right.

  Key:
  4. The noises of the train were irritating.
  5. The odor of the smokestacks was terrible.

Teaching Notes

To write the correct sentence, students transform the possessive word into a noun. They apply a rule that they have learned (lessons 35–41) about possessive words. To transform the word, write the part of the word that comes before the apostrophe. The possessive word in item 1 is **campers'.** The part before the apostrophe is **campers.** That's the correct noun. For item 2, the possessive word is **door's.** The part before the apostrophe is **door.** That's the correct noun.

If students write the wrong verb, have them say the original sentence. Then remind them, "You use the same verb in the transformed sentence."

SUBJECT-VERB AGREEMENT

In lesson 56, students work from sentences that have two nouns in the subject. Here's the exercise from the student textbook.

---

1. The tax on her purchases _____ two dollars.
2. The group of soldiers _____ resting.
3. The flights of our plane _____ exciting.

Teaching Notes

These items involve words other than **of.** Some of the items do not readily transform into possessive constructions. If students make mistakes, tell them, "The first noun is the main noun. That's the one you use to figure out the verb."

PASSIVE TO ACTIVE

In lesson 61, students learn how to transform passive sentences into active sentences. The sentences they work with name the actor.

Example: **The rabbits were fed by Alice.** Students first identify the actor (Alice). Then they rewrite the sentence so it names the actor and tells what the actor did: **Alice fed the rabbits.** Here are the items from lesson 61.

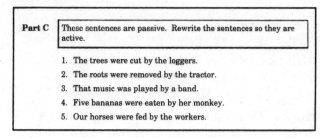

Part C These sentences are passive. Rewrite the sentences so they are active.

1. The trees were cut by the loggers.
2. The roots were removed by the tractor.
3. That music was played by a band.
4. Five bananas were eaten by her monkey.
5. Our horses were fed by the workers.

Teaching Notes

Students sometimes change the verb or other parts of the sentence when transforming it. For example, students might write this for item 3: **The band plays music** instead of **A band played that music.** To correct mistakes of this type, tell students: "You must use all the words in the original sentence except **was** and **by.** I see the word **a** in that sentence. You must use that word. I also see the word **that.** You must use that word." Do not permit students to write sloppy transformations.

For some sentences, the verb is irregular. For example, item 4: **Five bananas were eaten by her monkey.** If students have trouble with the correct verb, ask:

"Who is the actor in this sentence?" (Signal.) *Her monkey.*

"What did her monkey do?" (Signal.) *Ate five bananas.*

"Say the sentence that begins with **her monkey** and tells what her monkey did." (Signal.) *Her monkey ate five bananas.*

In lesson 67, students work with sentences that have an indefinite **they: The bank opened its new parking lot. They also gave away balloons.** To rewrite the underlined sentence, students first identify the actor. Who gave away balloons? The correct answer is **the bank.** Students write two possible sentences: **The bank also gave away balloons. It also gave away balloons.**

Teaching Notes

This activity is an extension of the analysis of who did the action. This analysis begins with the subject of the sentence, extends to subject-verb agreement, applies to transforming passive sentences to active ones, and concludes with the identification of a word to replace the indefinite **they.** Related activities are in the track labeled **General/Specific: Appropriate Category Words.** In that track, students identify a possible category name for the main thing that is referred to in a sentence.

General/Specific

The directions and descriptions that students rewrite involve the use of more general or more specific category words. The main activities that students do in the general/specific track are combining sentence parts that are more specific; critiquing deductions that are faulty because the conclusion is more general than the evidence; and creating appositives.

MORE GENERAL—MORE SPECIFIC

In the first lessons of the program (starting with lesson 1 and continuing through lesson 5), students identify the more specific parts of sentences. Here are the items from lesson 2.

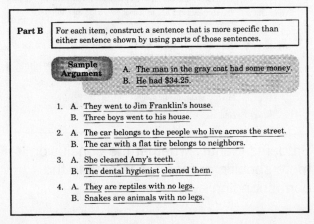

Part B   For each item, construct a sentence that is more specific than either sentence shown by using parts of those sentences.

Sample Argument
A. The man in the gray coat had some money.
B. He had $34.25.

1. A. They went to Jim Franklin's house.
   B. Three boys went to his house.

2. A. The car belongs to the people who live across the street.
   B. The car with a flat tire belongs to neighbors.

3. A. She cleaned Amy's teeth.
   B. The dental hygienist cleaned them.

4. A. They are reptiles with no legs.
   B. Snakes are animals with no legs.

Each item shows a pair of parallel sentences. Both refer to the same thing. One sentence has a more specific subject; the other has a more specific predicate. Students identify the subject that is more specific and the predicate that is more specific. Students then create a sentence more specific than either sentence shown by combining the more specific subject with the more specific predicate. Here's a sentence students create for item 1:
Three boys went to Jim Franklin's house.

In later lessons, students work with three parallel sentences and create the most specific possible sentence by combining the most specific subject and most specific predicate.

---

1. A. A young man studied history.
   B. A young person studied a subject.
   C. A male studied Canadian history.

Students write: **A young man studied Canadian history.**

Beginning in lesson 4, students identify whether the conclusion of a deduction is more specific or more general than the evidence. Here are items from lesson 4.

Argument 1:	Dan loves the smell of roses. Roses are flowers with thorns. Therefore, Dan loves the smell of all flowers with thorns.
Argument 2:	All arguments have a conclusion. Argument 2 is an argument. Therefore, argument 2 has a conclusion.
Argument 3:	All the residents of Homer Island are excellent fishermen. Jane Carter is a resident of Homer Island. Therefore, Jane Carter is an excellent fisherman.
Argument 4:	The students at Fenger School do well in all subjects. Music is a subject. Therefore, the students at Fenger School do well in music.
Argument 5:	Grace Brown is the best bike rider I know. Grace lives on Homer Island. Therefore, all the girls on Homer Island must be excellent bike riders.
Argument 6:	Ted did poorly in math. Math is an academic subject. Therefore, Ted must have done poorly in all academic subjects.

Students identify whether the conclusion is more specific or more general than the corresponding evidence.

Teaching Notes

If students are firm on the earlier work with general and specific, they should not have serious problems with this type of exercise. If they are not firm, however, they will not understand the basis for judging the conclusion of some arguments to be improper. Spurious arguments that have a conclusion more general than the evidence are very common. Understanding the problem with these arguments is very important for students. Therefore, make sure that students are firm on the earlier work with specific and general. If students are weak on any of the deduction items, repeat them.

DEFINITIONS

Starting in lesson 41, students create nonrestrictive clauses that define or describe. These clauses require students to identify category words that are specific enough to be useful.

Example: **They went on a galleon, which is a type of large sailing ship used in the years 1400 through 1700.**

Part D	For each item, use a dictionary and rewrite the sentence so it explains what the uncommon word means.

1. She rode a handsome Appaloosa.
2. Many European people enjoy borscht.
3. Everybody laughed over the clown's hoodoo.

---

2. Find part D.
 • For each item in part D, you'll use a dictionary. You won't copy exactly what the dictionary says. You'll explain what the uncommon word means so the reader would understand it.
3. Item 1: **She rode a handsome Appaloosa.**
 • Look up **Appaloosa.** Then rewrite the sentence so it tells what an **Appaloosa** is.

- Put that part just after the word **Appaloosa** in the sentence.
- Remember, make a comma and start with the words **which is.** Then summarize what an **Appaloosa** is and how it differs from other animals of the same type. Pencils down when you're finished.
  (Observe students and give feedback.)
- I'll read a good sentence. Listen: She rode a handsome Appaloosa, which is a hardy breed of horse developed by the Palouse Indians.
- Here's a sentence that is not as good: **She rode a handsome Appaloosa, which is a breed developed in the American West.**
- What's wrong with that sentence?
- (Call on a student. Idea: *It doesn't tell that the animal is a horse.*)
- (Call on several students to read their sentence. After each sentence is read, ask the class: **Does that sentence tell what an Appaloosa is? Does it tell something about how it is different from any other horse?** Praise sentences that follow the specified form and provide a good description.)
4. Item 2: **Many European people enjoy borscht.**
- Write the complete sentence. Remember, tell what borscht is and tell something about how it is different from other things like it. Pencils down when you're finished.
  (Observe students and give feedback.)
- Here's a good sentence: Many European people enjoy borscht, which is a cold soup made from beets and cabbage.
- Here's a sentence that is not too good: **Many European people enjoy borscht, which is a soup.**
- What's wrong with that sentence?
  (Call on a student. Idea: *It doesn't tell how it is different from other soups.*)

- (Call on several students to read their sentence. After each sentence is read, ask the class: **Does that sentence tell what borscht is? Does it tell something about how it is different from any other soup?** Praise sentences that follow the specified form and provide a good description.)
5. Item 3: **Everybody laughed over the clown's hoodoo.**
- Write the sentence that tells what **hoodoo** is. Pencils down when you're finished.
  (Observe students and give feedback.)
- Here's a good sentence: Everybody laughed over the clown's hoodoo, which is bad luck.
- (Call on different students to read their sentence. Praise sentences that explain **hoodoo.**)

Teaching Notes

This activity requires students to work in teams. Each team should have four students. Teams should be permanent assignments. At the beginning of the lesson, make sure that students are either seated in teams or are able to get to their teams without a lot of disruption. Teams should consist of students who are relatively homogeneous in skills. For lower performing groups, one student may be higher performing, but it's not a good idea for a group to have three higher performers and one lower performer. Ideally, each student would have a dictionary.

In step 3, teams look up the word **Appaloosa** and rewrite the sentence so it has a clause that begins with the words **which is.** The teams should discuss possible wording; however, it is not necessary for all students in the team to write the same sentence. Often all the students will write the same sentence.

Check to make sure that each student writes a sentence.

If teams have questions, students should raise their hands.

Do not permit students to spend a lot of time discussing or looking up the word. If students haven't located the word after a minute, tell them the page number for the word.

Note that this activity follows work with essential and nonessential clauses. Students have learned that the word **which** introduces a clause that is not essential. They have also learned that nonessential clauses are signalled with a comma. (See **Clarity of Meaning**.)

The clauses that students write must do two things—tell what an **Appaloosa** is and tell how it differs from other things in that class.

Here are sentences that are not acceptable:

She rode a handsome Appaloosa, which is a horse.

(Sentence doesn't tell the difference.)

She rode a handsome Appaloosa horse.

(Sentence doesn't follow the instructions.)

She rode a handsome Appaloosa, which is a special breed developed in the American west.

(Sentence doesn't tell the class that Appaloosas are in.)

Remind students, "You have to tell what it is and how it is different from things of the same type."

APPOSITIVES

Beginning in lesson 44, students work with items similar to those for definitions, but now they write appositives, truncated versions of nonessential clauses.

Instead of writing **which is a breed of horse developed in the American west,** students write **a breed of horse developed in the American west.** Here are the items from lesson 44:

1. The queen lost a frisette.
2. His samisen was very old.
3. Brian bought and sold suint.

Students follow the same rules that apply to other nonrestrictive elements. They insert the element after the name it refers to (not necessarily at the end of the sentence); they set if off with commas; they use wording that gives a clear description.

APPROPRIATE CATEGORY WORDS

In lesson 48, students work with items that clarify the need for category words that are specific. Items use very general category words:

The wadi, something that is open and usually dry, extended from the foothills to the plains.

Students look up **wadi** in the dictionary, identify a class name that is specific enough to make the original sentence clear and rewrite the original sentence:

The wadi, a valley that is open and usually dry, extended from the foothills to the plains.

The sentence now gives the reader a much more precise idea of what a **wadi** is. From the original sentence, the **wadi** could be anything from a train to a dust cloud. The rewritten sentence rules out these possibilities and not only indicates that it is a landform, but also specifies the type of landform.

Teaching Notes

The skills associated with these activities are thinking skills. They require students to make judgements. Help them out by presenting the appropriate tests. Here, the appropriate test is the clarity of the sentence they write. The original sentence is vague.

If some students use better words than others, point out why they are better: "Listen to these two parts. Tell me which part gives the better picture: a landform that is open and usually dry . . . a valley that is open and usually dry. . . ."

Also point out if words are not common: "an arroyo that is open and usually dry. That part may not help us make a very clear picture if we don't know what an arroyo is."

Finally, students work with sentences that give adequate category words but that do not tell anything specific about what is being described. This work begins in lesson 52. Here are the items from that lesson.

Part A	Copy each sentence and complete it by adding words that tell what is different about the unfamiliar word.

1. They had a pet mongoose, a carnivorous animal.
2. We wrote palindromes, which are words.
3. He had pictures of a serval, a cat.

Teaching Notes

As with the other activities in this track, this one requires selection. Students are not to copy the words from the definition. They are to select the words that make sense and that communicate.

For item 1, they must tell enough about a mongoose to indicate how it is different from other carnivorous animals. For this example, they could indicate that it lives in India, that it kills cobras, and that it looks like a weasel. Correct definitions that have redundant parts or unclear wording: . . . a pet mongoose, a carnivorous animal that is a pet and eats flesh. . . .

The words that students define are not important words. What is important, however, is the students' ability to identify the class (the general part of the definition) and the features (the specific part that differentiates that which is defined from others in the same class).

If students can reliably create acceptable sentences, they understand the sentence form and what the parts mean. This information is very important for both their future reading and writing.

Throughout the general/specific activities, students write complete sentences. Although this part of the activities may seem to waste time, it is very important. Students acquire the sense of nonfictional language by reading it and writing it. The sentences that they write serve as templates or patterns for efficient ways to express ideas that are often difficult for them to learn in other contexts. For instance, after completing this track, students have a feel for appositives and other nonessential clauses.

Clarity of Meaning

A major difference between careful writing and speaking is that careful writing must be precise and clear. It must also convey the intended meaning. Many writing conventions are driven by the need for precision and clarity of meaning.

In Level F, students work with various meaning-driven exercises. All of these exercises involve unintended meanings that students identify. Students work first with comparative sentences that have an unintended meaning: **The dog ate more than the cat.** (The sentence implies that the dog ate the cat.)

Students next work with descriptions of actions that are too vague to specify exactly what happened. **(She touched the striped triangle.** Problem: There is more than one striped triangle. Solution: **She touched the large striped triangle.)** A variation of this problem type involves inserting clauses. **(Tim's cat was in the grass.** Problem: There's more than one cat in the grass. Solution: **Tim's cat was in the grass that was long.)**

Similarly, in a later exercise, students edit directions that indicate how to construct a figure. The problem with the original directions is that they tell about constructing more than one of the figures shown in the set. The solution is to provide more detail, either with adjectives, phrases or clauses.

Students also work with ambiguous sentences that have the word **this** that is not followed by a noun and may therefore be unclear. Students identify an appropriate noun and rewrite the sentence.

Finally, students work with sentences that have a poor choice of verb. (**Her preference was sitting on the patio.** The unintended meaning is that her **preference** was sitting someplace.)

For all these exercises, students examine the sentence or item for both the intended meaning and a possible unintended meaning. The solution is to rewrite the item so it no longer has the unintended meaning. This specific search for meaning will provide students both the direction and the tools needed to write clearly and to critique arguments and proposals.

COMPARATIVES

In lesson 7, students make some sentences more parallel. This involves creating parallel forms of verbs or parallel phrases. Here are the items from lesson 7.

1. The dogs ran faster than the children.
2. Wayne suffered more from the cold than the wind.
3. They put more gas in the tractor than the truck.
4. The horse weighed more than the cow.
5. Diane crawls faster than Frances.
6. The wind blew faster from the west than the north.

Students add a parallel verb to the end of the sentence.

Item 1: **The dogs ran faster than the children ran.**

The next set of activities, from lesson 9, includes sentences that would have a silly meaning if they were made more parallel:

Part C Write the number of each sentence that would have a silly meaning if you rewrote it. Then rewrite the other sentences so that they are parallel.

1. Tina painted faster than her father.
2. Freddie ate less than the rest of the students.
3. Freddie ate less than a plateful.
4. Soo Lin lost more than ten dollars.
5. She walked faster to the store than the school.
6. Marie walked more than a mile.
7. More rain fell in the morning than the evening.
8. The lily smelled better than the rose.

1. Find part B.
   - I'll read what it says. Follow along:

   > - Some sentences that compare do not need wording that is perfectly parallel. In fact, perfectly parallel wording sometimes makes a silly meaning.
   > - You can see a sentence: **Linda lifted more than the barbells.**
   > - If we make the sentence parallel, it has a silly meaning: **Linda lifted more than the barbells lifted.**
   > - The meaning is silly because barbells don't lift.

2. Find part C.
   - Some of the sentences would be silly if you made them perfectly parallel.
3. Write the number of each sentence that would have a silly meaning if you rewrote it. Pencils down when you're finished.
   (Observe students and give feedback.)
4. Here's what you should have: Sentences **3, 4,** and **6** would have a silly meaning if you made them perfectly parallel.
   - If you made sentence 3 perfectly parallel, it would say: **Freddie ate less than a plateful ate.** Platefuls don't eat.
   - If you made sentence 4 perfectly parallel, what would it say? **(Call on a student.)** *Soo Lin lost more than 10 dollars lost.*
   - That meaning is silly. Dollars do not lose things.
   - If you made sentence 6 perfectly parallel, what would it say? **(Call on a student.)** *Marie walked more than a mile walked.*
   - Miles don't walk.
   - Raise your hand if you identified all the sentences that you should not change.
5. Your turn: Rewrite the other sentences. Pencils down when you're finished.
   (Observe students and give feedback.)

6. Find the key at the back of your book on page 310. ✔
   - That shows what you should have.
   - Raise your hand if you got all of them right.

   Key:
   1. *Tina painted faster than her father painted.*
   2. *Freddy ate less than the rest of the students ate.*
   5. *She walked faster to the store than to the school.*
   7. *More rain fell in the morning than in the evening.*
   8. *The lily smelled better than the rose smelled.*

Teaching Notes

Before this exercise, students have practiced writing sentences so they are more parallel. The emphasis in the present exercise is on when such rewriting is appropriate. For sentence 1 it is: **Tina painted faster than her father painted.** For sentence 3, making the parts of the sentence more parallel creates a silly meaning: **Freddie ate less than a plateful ate.**

If students make mistakes, present these tasks:

"Say the sentence with a parallel verb."

"Does that sentence have a silly meaning?"

If yes, "What's the silly meaning?"

Students may have trouble generating the parallel sentence for some of the items: **She walked faster to the store than the school.** Students should write: **She walked faster to the store than to the school.**

If students tend to have trouble with items, repeat the items later.

DESCRIPTIONS

Beginning in lesson 21, students write and edit descriptions of what somebody did. Here's the student material from lesson 21.

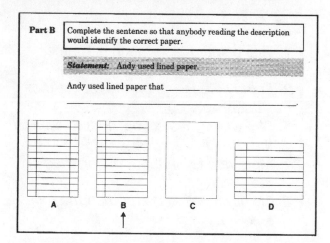

Students rewrite the original sentence so it has a clause that begins with **that.** The clause tells about the features of the object the arrow points to. This rewrite has two parts, one that distinguishes between B and A, the other that distinguishes between B and D. Here are appropriate sentences: **Andy used lined paper that has one margin. That paper is taller than it is wide.**

Teaching Notes

Students may write a variety of acceptable sentences or sentence pairs. Test the sentences: "Does that sentence rule out paper A? Does that sentence rule out paper D?" If the answer to both questions is yes, and if the sentences do not have serious grammatical problems, the description is acceptable.

Here are some of the acceptable sentence pairs: **Andy touched the paper that does not have two margins. That paper has 12 lines. (That paper is longer than it is wide.)**

Students are not permitted to describe papers by their position or letter. These descriptions are not acceptable: **Andy touched the paper that is labeled B. Andy touched the paper that is next to paper A. Andy touched the paper that is last in the row.** To correct such sentences: "Tell about some features of the object he touched."

Here are three of the items from lesson 23.

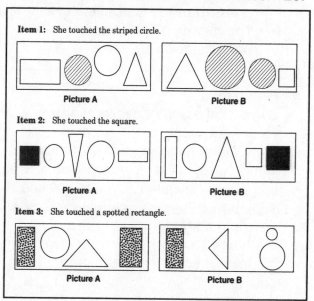

The description above the picture is adequate for one of the pictures but not the other. Students identify the letter of the picture that is adequately described. They then rewrite the item so it tells about the picture that has two similar objects.

For item 1, students would rewrite the sentence to tell about one of the circles in picture B. Possible sentences include: **She touched the larger striped circle; She touched the little striped circle.**

Teaching Notes

If students have trouble with this item, use this test: "Would somebody who read your sentence carefully know exactly which object she touched?"

Students work similar items in later lessons. In lesson 25, students do a variation in which the original sentence tells about two of three pictures. Students rewrite the sentence two ways. They remove a descriptor from the original sentence so that the sentence adequately describes only one of the pictures. Then they rewrite the sentence with an added descriptor so it tells about only one of the objects. Here's part of the exercise from lesson 25.

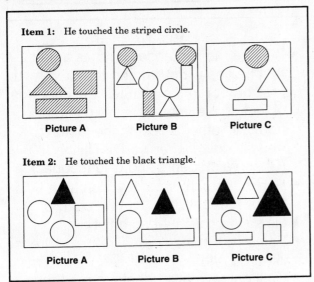

Item 1: He touched the striped circle.

Picture A   Picture B   Picture C

Item 2: He touched the black triangle.

Picture A   Picture B   Picture C

1. Each item has a sentence and three pictures.
   - The sentence is specific enough for **two** of those pictures.
2. Item 1: **He touched the striped circle.**
   - Write the letters of the two pictures that that sentence tells about. Pencils down when you're finished.
   (Observe students and give feedback.)
   - You should have written: **A** and **C.**
   - Now you're going to take a word **out** of the sentence so it tells about **only one** of those pictures.
   - Pencils down when you've written the sentence that tells about only one of the pictures in item 1.
   (Observe students and give feedback.)
   - Here's the sentence you should have: He touched the circle.
   - Which picture does that sentence tell about? (Signal.) *A.*

- You don't have to mention that it's striped because there's only one circle in picture A.
- Now you're going to write the sentence that is specific enough for picture B.
- Pick one of the striped circles in picture B. Write the sentence so it tells about that circle and none of the others. Pencils down when you've written a sentence that tells about B.
(Observe students and give feedback.)
- Here are some good sentences for B: He touched the striped circle that is on a triangle.
- Or: He touched the striped circle that is on a rectangle.
- (Call on several students to read their sentence. After each sentence, say: **From that sentence, would you know which object he touched in picture B?** Correct errors.)

In step 2, students rewrite the sentence so it tells about the picture with two similar objects (picture B). Students may describe the circle in a number of ways. Here would be acceptable descriptions:

He touched the striped circle that is on the left side of the box.

He touched the striped circle that touches a triangle.

He touched the striped circle that is on top of a triangle.

Accept a description that has unnecessary words, but point out that it has unnecessary words: **He touched the striped circle that is on top of a white triangle.** The word **white** is not needed.

Also accept sentences that tell where the triangle **was,** not **is: He touched the striped circle that was on a triangle.**

For each sentence, test it: "Does that sentence clearly tell which object he touched?" If yes, a sentence with no flagrant grammatical errors is acceptable.

ESSENTIAL AND NONESSENTIAL ELEMENTS
In lesson 27, students add clauses that begin with **who** or **that.** Here are rules for creating these sentences: If the thing being described is human, use the word **who.** If the thing being described is non-human, use **that.** Here's part of the exercise from lesson 27.

Item 1: He saw a car.

Item 2: He met a boy.

3. Item 1 says: **He saw a car.**
- Rewrite the sentence so it has a part that begins with **that** and tells about the **first object** in the picture. Describe that object so we know how it's different from any other object in the picture. Pencils down when you're finished. **(Observe students and give feedback.)**
- Here's the sentence rewritten so it tells about the first object in the picture:
‖ He saw a car that had a flat tire.
- Raise your hand if you wrote a sentence like that one.
- (Call on several students to read their sentence. Praise sentences that have the word **that** and describe the first car. After each sentence, ask: **Is that sentence specific enough to tell about the first object in the picture?)**

4. Item 2 says: **He met a boy.**
- Rewrite that sentence so it has a part that begins with **who** and tells about the first boy in the picture. Just tell what's different about that boy. Pencils down when you're finished. **(Observe students and give feedback.)**
- Here's the sentence rewritten so it tells about the first boy in the picture:
‖ He met a boy who was on a bicycle.
- Raise your hand if you wrote a sentence like that one.
- (Call on several students to read their sentence. Praise sentences that have the word **who** and describe the first boy. After each sentence, ask: **Is that sentence specific enough to tell about the first boy in the picture?)**

Teaching Notes

The test for sentences that students create is: "Is that sentence specific enough to tell about the first object in the picture?" By applying that test to item 1, you would accept a variety of sentences:

He saw a car that had a flat tire.

He saw a car that had a front tire that was flat.

He saw a car that had a flat.

These sentences are not acceptable:

He saw a car with a flat tire.

He saw the first car.

He saw that car that was left of the train.

To correct mistakes in which students describe the car by position: "Write about a feature of the car."

In lesson 29, students write a simple sentence for one of the pictures shown and a sentence with a **who** clause or a **that** clause for the picture with two similar objects.

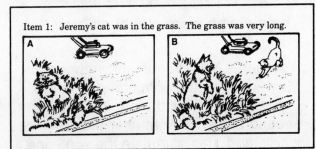

Item 1: Jeremy's cat was in the grass. The grass was very long.

For the preceding pictures, students write the first sentence for picture A. For picture B, they combine the two sentences: **Jeremy's cat was in the grass that was very long.** At this point, students are creating sentences that have essential clauses.

Students are introduced to nonessential clauses in lesson 33. The test: If a part that begins with **who** or **that** is not needed to make the sentence specific enough, that part is not needed. To show that the part is not needed, students set that part off with commas. Here's part of the introduction.

4. The combined sentence for item 1 is: **The boy who has short hair is always late.**
- Look at the picture. How many boys are there? (Signal.) *One.*
- So you don't need the combined sentence.
- You'll use commas to set off the part of the sentence that is not needed.
- Copy the combined sentence for item 1 and show the commas. Pencils down when you're finished.
(Observe students and give feedback.)
- (Write on the board:)

> 1. The boy, who has short hair, is always late.

- Here's what you should have: **The boy, comma, who has short hair, comma, is always late.**
- Listen to how you would say the sentence: The boy, who has short hair, is always late.
- Raise your hand if you got it right.

5. Item 2. The combined sentence is not needed. Write the combined sentence for item 2. Set off the part that is not essential with commas. Pencils down when you're finished.

   (Observe students and give feedback.)
- (Write on the board:)

   2. The children, who wore black T-shirts, played softball.

- Here's the sentence you should have: **The children, comma, who wore black T-shirts, comma, played softball.**
- Listen to that sentence: The children, who wore black T-shirts, played softball.
- Raise your hand if you wrote that sentence and punctuated it properly.

6. Find part D.
- For one of the pictures, the combined sentence is needed. You'll write that sentence with **no commas.**
- For the other picture, the combined sentence is not needed. You'll write that sentence with commas to mark the part that is not essential.

7. Write the combined sentence for each picture. Pencils down when you're finished.

   (Observe students and give feedback.)
- Here's what you should have for picture A:
   The girl, comma, who wore number 17, comma, ran 3 miles.
- The sentence for picture B has no commas because we need the information about her number to know which girl the sentence refers to.
   You should have written:
   The girl who wore number 17 ran 3 miles.
- Raise your hand if you wrote the correct sentence for each picture.

- (Call on several students.) Read your sentence for picture A. Pause to indicate the part that is not essential.

Teaching Notes

In steps 5 and 7, you check students' sentences. Students may not combine sentences appropriately. The rules for combining are:

Find the part that is the same in both sentences.

Touch that part in the first sentence.

Insert the second sentence right after that part.

Start with the word **who** or **that** in place of the subject.

For part C, item 2, the common part is the words **the children.** The second sentence goes right after the words **the children** in the first sentence. For part D, picture B, the common part is **the girl.** The second sentence is inserted right after the words **the girl** in the first sentence.

The girl [insert here] ran 3 miles.

The girl who wore number 17 ran 3 miles.

If students have trouble, have them put their finger on the common part in the first sentence. Tell them to insert the second sentence right after those words and then complete the sentence.

Here are some of the mistakes that students make in trying to combine the sentences:

The children played softball who wore black T-shirts.

The children played softball, they wore black T-shirts.

The children who wore black T-shirts.

The children who played softball wore black T-shirts.

Do not permit any of these errors to be uncorrected. The second sentence is inserted in the first. No variations are permitted. If students write, **The children who played softball wore black T-shirts,** the sentence is correct with punctuation because the first sentence in the item does not say, **The children wore black T-shirts.** It says, **The children played softball.** That's what the final sentence must say.

If students have trouble with this exercise, make sure they have clear information about what is acceptable. Then have them repeat the exercise.

In lesson 36, the pronoun **which** is introduced. The word **which** replaces the word **that** if the clause is not essential. The word **which** is not appropriate if the clause is essential. Here's part of the introduction from lesson 36.

---

1. *Here's an essential part:*
   She has an old bike.
   Here's a part you want to add:
   The bike is red and white.

2. *Here's an essential part:*
   She has an old bike.
   Here's another essential part:
   That bike is red and white.

3. *Here's an essential part:*
   She wanted to buy a camera.
   Here's another essential part:
   That camera cost $450.

4. *Here's an essential part:*
   Her camera takes wonderful pictures.
   Here's a part you want to add:
   That camera is on sale at Z-Mart.

5. *Here's an essential part:*
   That train gets here at 6 a.m.
   Here's a part you want to add:
   That train comes from Chicago.

---

3. Item 1. Here's an essential part: **She has an old bike.**
- Here's a part you want to add: **The bike is red and white.**

- Write the combined sentence. Remember what to do for the part that is not essential. Use a comma and a particular word. Pencils down when you're finished.
  (Observe students and give feedback.)
- (Write on the board:)

> **1. She has an old bike, which is red and white.**

- Here's what you should have: **She has an old bike, which is red and white.** The part that is not essential begins with a comma and has the word **which**.
4. Item 2. Here's an essential part: **She has an old bike.**
- Here's another essential part: **That bike is red and white.**
- For this item, the second part is essential.
- Write the combined sentence. Pencils down when you're finished.
  (Observe students and give feedback.)
- (Write on the board:)

> **2. She has an old bike that is red and white.**

- Here's what you should have: **She has an old bike that is red and white.**
5. Write the combined sentence for item 3. Pencils down when you're finished.
  (Observe students and give feedback.)
- (Write on the board:)

> **3. She wanted to buy a camera that cost $450.**

- Here's what you should have: **She wanted to buy a camera that cost $450.** There's no comma because the part is essential. It begins with the word **that.** You'd use that part if there's more than one camera.
6. Your turn: Write the combined sentences for the rest of the items in part D. Pencils down when you're finished.
  (Observe students and give feedback.)

Teaching Notes

Each item tells whether the second part is essential. If it is, the part is inserted right after the common part in the first sentence, using the word **that**. If it is not essential, it is inserted in the same place, using a comma and the word **which**.

Students may have trouble with items 4 and 5. They are to insert the second sentence after the common part appears in the first sentence:

4. Her camera [insert here] takes wonderful pictures.

Her camera, which is on sale at Z-Mart, takes wonderful pictures.

5. That train [insert here] gets here at 6 a.m.

That train, which comes from Chicago, gets here at 6 a.m.

AMBIGUOUS ADJECTIVES

In lesson 64, students are introduced to constructions that are ambiguous because of the placement of an adjective.

Example: **They collected old coins and jewels.**

Were the jewels old? Maybe. If they were, the sentence could be rewritten this way: **They collected old coins and old jewels.** If the jewels weren't old, the sentence could be rewritten this way: **They collected jewels and old coins.** Students rewrite items of this type for each possibility. Here's part of the exercise from lesson 64.

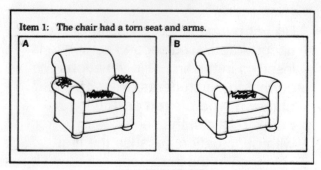

Item 1: The chair had a torn seat and arms.

- These sentences are sort of parallel. You're going to rewrite them two ways, one way for each meaning.
3. Sentence 1: **The chair had a torn seat and arms.**
- That sentence could refer to picture A or picture B. What's torn in picture A? **(Signal.)** *Seat and arms.*
- What's torn in picture B? **(Signal.)** *Seat.*
- The chair in picture B has arms, but they are not torn. So that chair has a torn seat, and it has arms.
- Rewrite the original sentence so it tells about picture A. Make the parts more parallel. Pencils down when you're finished.

  (Observe students and give feedback.)
- **(Write on the board:)**

  > 1. The chair had a torn seat and torn arms.

- Here's a good sentence: **The chair had a torn seat and torn arms.**
- Or you could have written:
  The chair had a torn seat and had torn arms.
- **(Call on several students to read their sentence. Praise good sentences.)**
- Now rewrite the sentence so it tells about picture B. Make it clear. Pencils down when you're finished.

  (Observe students and give feedback.)
- **(Write to show:)**

  > 1. The chair had a torn seat and torn arms.
  >
  > The chair had arms and a torn seat.

- Here's what you should have for picture B: **The chair had arms and a torn seat.** Raise your hand if you wrote that sentence.
- (Call on several students to read their sentence. Praise good sentences.)

At the same time that students work on rewriting sentences that have a possible ambiguous meaning because of the order, they also rewrite sentences that have a "naked" this or that (without a noun following it). Here's part of the exercise from lesson 64.

---

1. They decided to complain about the noise. They wanted this to cause some action.

2. They finally decided to buy the mountain bike. It took them two weeks to arrive at this.

3. Tom recommended that we should bring along work clothes. Randy did not agree with this.

---

4. Item 1: **They decided to complain about the noise. They wanted this to cause some action.**
- The word **this** doesn't name the thing that would cause the action.
- Write the sentence with the name after **this.** Pencils down when you're finished. (Observe students and give feedback.)
- Here's a good sentence:
  They wanted this complaint to cause some action.
- The word **complaint** is better than **complaining.**
5. Item 2: **They finally decided to buy the mountain bike. It took them two weeks to arrive at this.**
- Write the sentence so it has a name after **this.** Pencils down when you're finished. (Observe students and give feedback.)
- Here's a good sentence:
  It took them two weeks to arrive at this decision.
- (Call on several students to read their sentence. Praise good sentences.)

6. Item 3: **Tom recommended that we should bring along work clothes. Randy did not agree with this.**
- Fix up the sentence. Pencils down when you're finished. (Observe students and give feedback.)
- Here's a good sentence:
  Randy did not agree with this recommendation.
- Or you could have written: **Randy did not agree with this proposal** or **this plan** or **this idea.** Any of those names are fine.
- (Call on several students to read their sentence. Praise good sentences.)

Teaching Notes

The noun that students select may be related to the verb in the first sentence, and it may be unrelated. Here are some possible words for item 1: **complaint; complaining;** possibly **decision** (but this meaning is not as direct as one related to complaining); **choice; deed; idea; plan.**

When students read their sentence, ask them whether the sentence is clear.

AMBIGUOUS VERBS

In lesson 66, students are introduced to ambiguities that are created by the form of the verb.

Milton's thought was making a new fence.

The sentence indicates that Milton's thought had fence-construction skills. The sentence can be rewritten three ways: With **that— Milton's thought was <u>that</u> we should make a new fence.** Another way is to change the verb form: **Milton's thought <u>was to make</u> a new fence.** The third way is to change the noun into a verb: <u>**Milton thought**</u> **that we should build a new fence.** Here is part of the introduction.

1. Somebody asked where we preferred to eat dinner. <u>Brenda's preference was sitting on the patio.</u>

2. Somebody asked how we would pay for the repairs. <u>Ms. Wilson's feeling was borrowing money.</u>

3. Item 1 is a response to what somebody asked: **Somebody asked where we preferred to eat dinner. Brenda's preference was sitting on the patio.**

• I hope her **preference** does not get too cold out there.

• Rewrite the sentence so it has the verb that tells **to do something.** Don't change the meaning of the sentence. Pencils down when you're finished. **(Observe students and give feedback.)**

• (Write on the board:)

> **1. Brenda's preference was to sit on the patio.**

• You should have a sentence like this one: **Brenda's preference was to sit on the patio.** That sentence is clear. Raise your hand if you got it right.

• (Call on several students to read their sentence. Praise good sentences.)

• Now you'll rewrite the original sentence so you don't use the noun **preference.** You'll exchange **preference** for the verb that is related to **preference.** Everybody, what verb is that? (Signal.) *Preferred.*

• Pencils down when you've rewritten the sentence. (Observe students and give feedback.)

• (Write to show:)

> **1. Brenda's preference was to sit on the patio.**
>
> **Brenda preferred sitting on the patio.**

• Here's the sentence you could have: **Brenda preferred sitting on the patio.** Or you could have something like: **Brenda preferred to sit on the patio.** Or: **Brenda preferred for us to sit on the patio.**

• (Call on several students to read their sentence. Praise good sentences.)

Teaching Notes

Expect students to have trouble generating some words, like **preferred.** If they have trouble, test them on it later: "Earlier in the lesson, you wrote a verb that is related to the noun **preference.** Everybody, what's the verb?" Point out to students that the difference between people who are fluent with written language and those who aren't has to do with their ability to generate words like **preferred.**

The various activities students do in the meaning of clarity track require very strict writing practices. Point out to students that in their personal writing, they may not always follow these strict rules. That's okay, so long as students know what the rules are and know how to write in a pristine manner if they need to communicate precisely.

Deductions and Inferences

In Level F, students engage in exercises that reinforce the notion that there are rules. Rules apply to a range of examples. Therefore, rules can be used as a basis for deductions.

Rules can also be formulated and modified on the basis of observations. This type of inference relates to the scientific method. The rules that we use in science provide the best explanation of the facts that we have and make the most accurate predictions that we know how to make. As information increases, we change the rules. Then we are more accurate in dealing with the examples. Sometimes, the information we receive forces a complete reconstruction of rules. (Space probes of planets like Mars provided information that led to rejection of many notions about the nature and structure of moons.)

Associated with this use of rules as "premises" for deductions are the possible violations. One might set up the deduction so it is faulty. One might try to draw conclusions where the evidence does not permit such conclusions.

Level F presents a series of exercises that relate to all these aspects of deductions and inferences. The work is further expanded in what students do in their writing.

DRAWING CONCLUSIONS FROM STATEMENTS OF EVIDENCE

The first deduction exercise appears in lesson 1. Students combine two statements of "evidence" to draw a conclusion. Here's part of the introduction from lesson 1.

Item 1: All gasoline engines have exhaust manifolds.
VMX engines are gasoline engines.

Item 2: Doris is more insidious than Clara.
Clara is more insidious than Denny.

Item 3: The magazine is more terse than the newspaper article.
The newspaper article is more terse than the record.

2. Find part G. Each argument shows the evidence. You're going to write the conclusion that follows from this evidence.

3. Item 1: **All gasoline engines have exhaust manifolds. VMX engines are gasoline engines.**
- Remember, the conclusion has parts of each sentence in the evidence, but it tells something that is not said in the evidence. And if the evidence is true, the sentence you'll write for the conclusion will be true. Your conclusion will start with the words **therefore, VMX engines.**

- Write the conclusion. Pencils down when you're finished.
(Observe students and give feedback.)
- (Write on the board:)

1. Therefore, VMX engines have exhaust manifolds.

- Here's the sentence you should have: **Therefore, VMX engines have exhaust manifolds.**
4. Item 2: **Doris is more insidious than Clara. Clara is more insidious than Denny.**
- You can draw a proper conclusion even if you don't know what **insidious** means.
- Write the conclusion that starts with the words **therefore, Doris.** Pencils down when you're finished.
(Observe students and give feedback.)
- (Write on the board:)

2. Therefore, Doris is more insidious than Denny.

- That conclusion has to be true if the evidence is true. Raise your hand if you got it right.
5. Item 3: **The magazine article is more terse than the newspaper article. The newspaper article is more terse than the record.**
- You can draw a proper conclusion even if you don't know what **terse** means.
- Write the conclusion that starts with the words **therefore, the magazine article.** Pencils down when you're finished.
(Observe students and give feedback.)
- (Write on the board:)

3. Therefore, the magazine article is more terse than the record.

- That conclusion has to be true if the evidence is true. Raise your hand if you got it right.

6. All your conclusions are true, but you probably don't know what the conclusions refer to.
- Raise your hand if you know what a **sora** is, what **manifolds** are, or what **insidious** and **terse** mean. (Call on several students.)
7. Find the key at the back of your book on page 310. ✔
- That shows what each of the things is.
  Key:
  > Sample: A sora is a small, short-billed rail of North America.
  1. A manifold is a chamber having several outlets through which a liquid or gas is distributed or gathered.
  2. An insidious person or thing looks harmless but actually causes harm.
  3. Something terse is straight to the point without apology.

Teaching Notes

The items are purposely designed so that students don't know the meaning of the words. The reason is that deductions are purely "mechanical" or procedural. The subject of one piece of evidence is combined with the predicate of the other to form a conclusion. If students are to become facile with deductions, they must learn the "sound" or feel of them.

At the end of the exercise, students refer to a key that indicates what the words mean. If the words that are used in a deduction have a meaning, the conclusion follows from the evidence. If students complain that they don't know the meaning of the words, tell them, "You don't have to know what they mean to draw a conclusion. Draw the conclusion."

DISCREDITING RULES

In lesson 4, students are introduced to the notion that a person's experiences may result in greatly different knowledge or rules. The items give a rule and a set of examples. Not all examples follow the rule. Two different people examine the examples. One concludes that the examples support the rule. The other person concludes that the examples discredit the rule. Here is part of the exercise from lesson 4.

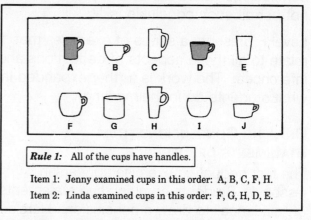

Rule 1: All of the cups have handles.

Item 1: Jenny examined cups in this order: A, B, C, F, H.

Item 2: Linda examined cups in this order: F, G, H, D, E.

2. Item 1. The rule for item 1 is: **All of the cups have handles.**
- The cups are lettered.
- Below is the set of cups that Jenny examined. She didn't examine all of them before drawing her conclusion. She examined cups **A, B, C, F,** and **H.**
- Look at the cups she examined and then see whether her observations support the rule or discredit the rule about the cups. If all the cups she looked at have handles, her observations would support the rule. If some of them do not have handles, her observations would discredit the rule. Remember, the rule indicates that all the cups have handles.
- Write about Jenny's observations. Write, **Jenny's observations support the rule,** or, **Jenny's observations discredit the rule.** Pencils down when you're finished.

(Observe students and give feedback.)

- You should have written:
‖ Jenny's observations support the rule.
- All the cups that she examined have handles. The rule is: **All the cups have handles.** So her observations support the rule.
3. Do item 2. See whether Linda's observations support the rule or discredit it. Write your sentence about Linda's observations. Pencils down when you're finished.
(Observe students and give feedback.)
- Did Linda's observations support the rule or discredit it? (Signal.) *Discredit it.*
- You should have written:
‖ Linda's observations discredit the rule.
4. Linda observed five cups. She didn't have to examine all five cups before she knew that the rule about the cups was false.
- Start with the first cup she examined— that's cup **F**—and write the letters of the cups she examined until she first knew that the rule was false. Pencils down when you're finished.
- (Write on the board:)

F   G

- Here's what you should have written. She knew that the rule was false after she examined cup **G**. You should have written: **F** and **G**. She did not need any more observations to discredit the rule.

Students do exercises in which they indicate what sort of evidence would be needed to discredit a rule. How many examples are needed? (Generally one.) How is that example different from others that support the rule? (The example does not have features the rule says it must have.)

In lesson 13, students work with a series of rules and examples. The rules are about creatures in a strange place. The actual creatures that students examine discredit some of the rules. Here is part of the work from lesson 13.

Here are the rules:
1. All creatures with an eye have a tail.
2. All creatures with a tail have an eye.
3. All creatures with a pointed top have eyelashes.

Questions
1. Which of the creatures you examined does rule 1 tell about?
2. Which of the creatures discredits rule 1?
3. Why does that creature discredit the rule?

4. Which of the creatures you examined does rule 2 tell about?
5. Which of the creatures discredits rule 2?

6. Which of the creatures you examined does rule 3 tell about?
7. Which of the creatures discredits rule 3?
8. Why does that creature discredit the rule?

Here are the creatures

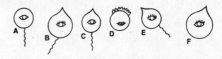

Teaching Notes

Students are to answer questions that may seem obvious but that aren't.

The first question is, **Which of the creatures you examined does rule ___ tell about?** The first part of the rule names the creatures. For rule 1: All creatures with an eye have a tail. Rule 1 tells about all creatures with an eye. Rule 1 does not tell about all creatures with a tail.

The next question is, **Which of the creatures discredits rule _____ ?** To discover whether any creatures discredit the rule, students first examine all of the creatures the rule tells about.

Rule 1 tells about creatures with an eye. Therefore, students examine all the creatures with an eye. Students ask about each one: Does it have a tail? If every creature that has an eye also has a tail, no creature discredits the rule. If a creature that has an eye does not have a tail, that creature discredits the rule. That creature shows that **not all** creatures that have an eye have a tail.

Make sure that students are very accurate in evaluating the various examples. If they have trouble, repeat the exercise. Make sure students can identify what each rule tells about and can identify the examples the rule covers.

Students (and adults) are frequently confused by what rules purport to say. The rule **All Tindal socks are made of wool** does not imply that they are the only socks made of wool or that all socks made of wool are Tindal socks. To analyze the rule you ask, "What does the rule tell about?" Then you test those examples to see if what the rule says about those examples is true.

In later lessons, students test different rules.

CONSTRUCTING RULES FROM OBSERVATIONS

In lesson 16, students construct rules. Here is part of the exercise.

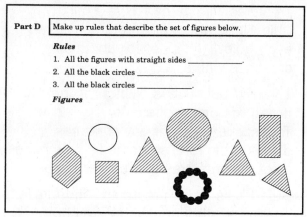

Part D | Make up rules that describe the set of figures below.

Rules
1. All the figures with straight sides _____.
2. All the black circles _____.
3. All the black circles _____.

Figures

1. Find part D.
   - These are figures. You're going to make up rules.

2. The first rule is for all the figures with straight sides.
   - Examine those figures. Write your rule. Pencils down when you're finished.
   (Observe students and give feedback.)
   - (Write on the board:)

   > **1. All the figures with straight sides have stripes.**

   - Here's a good rule: **All the figures with straight sides have stripes.** Raise your hand if you wrote a rule like that one.
   - (Call on several students to read their rule. Praise rules that express the idea: **All the figures with straight sides {have stripes/are striped}.**)

3. Now you're going to write two different rules for all the circles that are black.
   - Figure out two different things you can say about all those circles. Write two rules. Pencils down when you're finished.
   (Observe students and give feedback.)
   - (Write on the board:)

   > **All the black circles are touching each other.**
   > **All the black circles are in a ring.**
   > **All the black circles are small.**

   - Here are some good rules. You could have any two of them:
   | All the black circles are touching each other.
   | All the black circles are in a ring.
   | All the black circles are small.
   - Raise your hand if you wrote about the size. ✔
   - Raise your hand if you wrote about the fact that they're touching. ✔
   - Raise your hand if you wrote about the ring or the circle that they form. ✔
   - (Call on several students to read their rules. Praise pairs of rules that refer to two different features of the black circles.)

Teaching Notes

In step 2, students write their rules for figures with straight sides. If they write, **All the figures with straight sides are either triangles or rectangles,** ask the group, "Is there a figure that discredits that rule?"

Use a similar strategy to test the adequacy of rules that students generate. If there is no example that discredits the rule, it's acceptable.

In lesson 22, students are introduced to rules about groups. If the statement or rule tells about the whole group and not about every individual in the group, evidence about one individual will not discredit the statement. Here are examples from lesson 22.

---

1. Every player on the Tigers is over six feet tall.
2. The Tigers eat over 60 pounds of vegetables every day.
3. The official uniform of the Tigers is red and gold.

Statement 1 is not about the team. It can be discredited by evidence about one individual. Statement 2 is about the team. It can be discredited only by evidence about the team. Statement 3 is about the team. It cannot be discredited by evidence about an individual. The problem that students have is determining whether the statement tells about the group or the individual. If students have trouble with an item, repeat it later.

CONSISTENCY

In lesson 25, students are introduced to consistency. In the context of rules, some possibilities seem consistent with rules. These possibilities may not be the actual ones that occur; however, they are the ones that would be predicted by the rules. Here are some of the items from lesson 25.

Item 1. *Facts:* Mr. Taylor is 80 years old. He has 7 married children. The oldest is 52. The youngest is 34.

    A. Mr. Taylor has no grandchildren.

    B. Mr. Taylor has many grandchildren.

    C. Mr. Taylor has one grandchild.

Item 2. *Facts:* It is now June. There was a great deal of rain this spring. The rain continued throughout the month of May.

    A. There is practically no danger of forest fires.

    B. There is a great danger of forest fires.

    C. The forest fires occurred in April, and there are no forests left in the area.

Item 3. *Facts:* Mrs. Anderson loves plants. For 26 years, she worked in a florist shop. She has a large home with an enormous backyard.

    A. She has a tiny garden.

    B. She has no garden at all.

    C. She has a large, beautiful garden.

Teaching Notes

Each of the choices is a possibility. Possibly, Mr. Taylor has no grandchildren; possibly, he has only one; possibly, he has many. If students have trouble with these items, ask, "What would you expect for a person who has seven married children?"

In this lesson and in later ones, students make up a theory to show that even more unlikely possibilities could occur. Students also make examples consistent with a fact or information.

Here are examples from lesson 27:

Part E Make up house prices that are consistent with the information given in the pictures.

① _____   ② $70,000

③ _____   ④ _____

The fact shows that the nicest of the modest homes costs $70,000. Given this information, students are to make up prices for the other houses. The prices must be consistent with the fact. A modest, well-maintained house in a good neighborhood costs $70,000. Therefore, the same house in a poorer neighborhood or in poorer condition would cost less. A more lavish house in a nice neighborhood would cost more. The consistency inferences are extended to a variety of features. Here is an example from lesson 28.

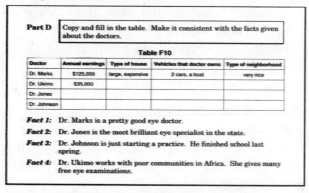

Part D Copy and fill in the table. Make it consistent with the facts given about the doctors.

Table F10

Doctor	Annual earnings	Type of house	Vehicles that doctor owns	Type of neighborhood
Dr. Marks	$125,000	large, expensive	2 cars, a boat	very nice
Dr. Ukimo	$35,000			
Dr. Jones				
Dr. Johnson				

Fact 1: Dr. Marks is a pretty good eye doctor.
Fact 2: Dr. Jones is the most brilliant eye specialist in the state.
Fact 3: Dr. Johnson is just starting a practice. He finished school last spring.
Fact 4: Dr. Ukimo works with poor communities in Africa. She gives many free eye examinations.

The facts tell about the "status" of the various doctors. Students use Dr. Marks as a benchmark for possessions the other doctors might have. The test for these items is whether the student is consistent.

Dr. Johnson should have less of everything than Dr. Marks but more of everything than Dr. Ukimo. If students indicate that Dr. Johnson has a house that is larger and expensive, ask what his salary is. (His salary should be less than that of Marks but more than Ukimo's. If his salary is less than that of Marks, his house should cost less than that of Marks.) Remind students, "You have to be consistent."

Writing

Students do a variety of writing exercises in Level F. The writing assignments dovetail with work that students do on tool skills. For example, after students learn a discrimination associated with specific/general, they do a series of writing assignments that incorporate the skill. After students have learned rules about deductions involving groups and what kind of evidence supports and discredits conclusions about groups, they do writing assignments in which they respond to faulty arguments involving groups and individuals. After students work on following directions, they do writing assignments in which they identify problems with written directions or descriptions.

Part of nearly every lesson in Level F involves outline diagrams. These diagrams provide model sentences for expressing different ideas. The major outline diagrams that are used in this program appear at the back of the student textbook. The first section shows the parts that are combined in the various diagrams. Each part is a particular icon that keys particular wording. This icon:

is a pair of X boxes. The X denotes disagreement.

This icon:

is a symbol for source. It indicates that the student is to refer to the source of information that the student is using.

Here are the diagrams for critiquing **different types of arguments.**

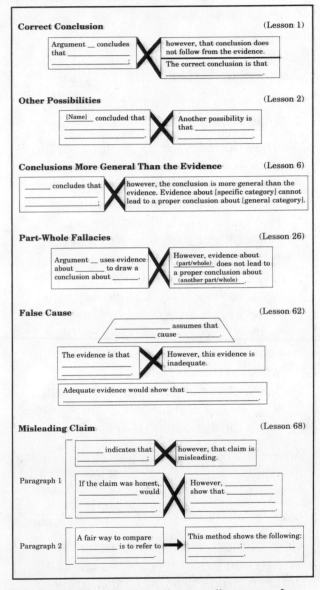

The following display shows diagrams for writing about **more than one requirement, rule testing, comparing** and **contrasting,** and **contradictions.**

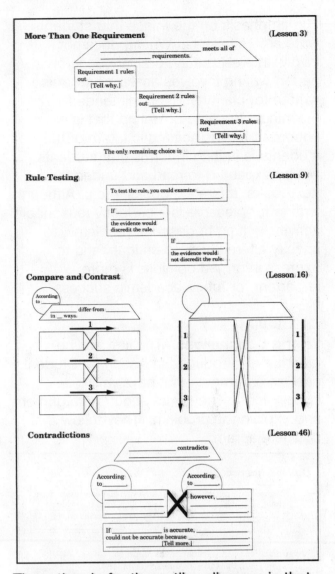

The rationale for the outline diagram is that students learn to use the language of exposition (not the language of everyday verbal exchanges and stories) by using that language correctly. The outline diagram serves as a template that gives students practice using the appropriate language. It makes the task of organizing the information easier; it assures that the students receive sufficient practice in writing variations of sentences that will serve them throughout their lives. Furthermore, the outline diagram is one of the few vehicles that provides such practice.

The emphasis on the things that students write are as follows: Writing does not involve merely putting oral language on paper; writing involves analyzing what is written for clarity and for unintended meanings; the type of writing that is most important for the academic future of the students is writing in forms that students will be expected to read and understand (textbooks, reference books, etc.). Although writing for pleasure is a perfectly reasonable activity, writing to describe problems, to specify alternatives, to critique, and to express informed opinions is more important for future academic success.

CRITIQUING

Wrong Conclusions. The first outline diagram is introduced in lesson 1. Students analyze arguments that have wrong conclusions. They write about the argument and explain the problem. They follow this outline diagram:

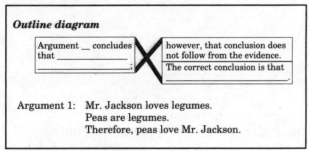

Here's part of the exercise from lesson 1.

4. Argument 1: **Mr. Jackson loves legumes. Peas are legumes. Therefore, peas love Mr. Jackson.**

- Write your paragraph about argument 1. Remember to follow all the wording shown in the outline diagram. Pencils down when you're finished.

    (Observe students and give feedback.)

- Here's a good paragraph:
  Argument 1 concludes that peas love Mr. Jackson; however, that conclusion does not follow from the evidence. The correct conclusion is that Mr. Jackson loves peas.

- Raise your hand if you wrote a paragraph just like the one I read.
- Make sure that you have the word **that** in your first sentence: **Argument 1 concludes that.** Make sure you have the semicolon before the word **however,** and a comma after the word **however.**
- (Call on several students to read their paragraph. Praise paragraphs that follow the outline diagram. Correct any deviations in wording.)

Teaching Notes

Here are the more common mistakes that students make:

1. They don't follow the wording of the outline diagram. They might write something like this: **The argument says peas love Mr. Jackson. However, Mr. Jackson loves peas.** Reject that response. Students are to follow the wording precisely. Direct students who make this mistake: "You have to do what the directions tell you to do. Follow the outline diagram and describe the problem with the argument. Use the wording that is shown."

2. They physically separate the parts they write (as if following the spatial rules for the outline diagram):

Argument 1 concludes that peas love Mr. Jackson; however, that conclusion does not follow from the evidence. The correct conclusion is that Mr. Jackson loves peas.

Correct these errors by pointing out: "When you follow the outline diagram, you just write paragraphs the way you normally would. The diagram shows you the wording. But what you write is in regular paragraph form."

3. When students indicate what the argument concludes, they include the word **therefore: Argument 1 concludes that therefore, peas love Mr. Jackson.** Correct by saying, "When you repeat the conclusion, you use the word **therefore.** When you indicate **what the argument concludes,** you don't need the word **therefore.**

4. Students omit the word **that: Argument 1 concludes peas love Mr. Jackson.** Correct by saying, "If you tell the exact words that the conclusion says, you'll write, **Argument 1 concludes *that* peas love Mr. Jackson.** Write the exact words in the conclusion." Show students:

- You can write about the conclusion two ways. One way has quotes.
- (Write on the board:)

Argument 1 concludes, "Peas love Mr. Jackson"; however . . .

Argument 1 concludes that peas love Mr. Jackson; however . . .

- If you write the conclusion the second way, you need the word **that.** If you don't have the word **that,** you must show quotes. The outline diagram does not call for quotes. Write it the second way. Note that in later lessons, the word **that** is dropped from the outline boxes; nevertheless, students should continue to use **that** or quotes.

5. Students do not punctuate the sentence properly. The word **however** is not capitalized in this sentence. It is preceded by a semicolon and followed by a comma. Make sure that students follow these punctuation conventions.

6. Students don't indicate what the correct conclusion is. They write something like, **The correct conclusion is different,** or, **The correct conclusion tells what he loves.**

When you show the correct work for an item, make sure that students fix up any mistakes. Remind them, "You have to attend to little details if you want to write correctly. Make sure you have all the words spelled correctly and all the punctuation correct." Also, make sure that you tell the students about the problem with the original argument. If students understand how they are to write early in the program, they will have far fewer problems when they work with more elaborate outline diagrams.

Remember, the part of the exercise in which you call on students to read their passage may be the most important part. It shows both possible mistakes and what sort of standards you are using for student writing. The more you provide this kind of feedback to the group, the more the students will see the variety of mistakes that are possible and learn how to avoid them.

INVALID ARGUMENTS

Other Possibilities. In lesson 2, students are introduced to an outline diagram that requires them to generate a possibility other than the one shown in an argument. Here's the outline diagram and one of the items from lesson 2.

Item 1

Irma lives two blocks from the ocean. One day, she saw her brother coming home. He was soaking wet. The sky was dark in the distance, and the streets were wet. Irma said to herself, "My brother got caught in the rain."

Outline diagram

| [Name] concluded that _____ _____. | ✗ | Another possibility is that _____ _____. |

Teaching Notes

Make sure that students follow the basic conventions for outline diagrams (writing in paragraphs, following the wording, and expressing ideas that are clear). The most common error students make is presenting possibilities that are not consistent with the evidence. For example: **Irma concluded that her brother got caught in the rain. Another possibility is that her brother fell off a ship.** At best, this conclusion is marginal. Point out: "All you know is what the item says. If the item does not tell about a ship, you can't refer to a ship unless you know there is one near Irma's house. Here's something you could write: **Another possibility is that he fell off a boat that was docked at a pier.** The best bet is to use the evidence that is given. All ocean shores have water. All have a shoreline. All have waves. Not all of them have ships."

Another problem that students have is using the wrong possessive adjectives. Example: **Irma concluded that my brother got caught in the rain.** Ask, "Whose brother got caught in the rain—yours or Irma's? That's her brother. That's what you say when you write sentences with the word **that:** Irma concluded **that** her brother got caught in the rain."

Again, make sure that students fix up questionable sentences and rewrite sentences that are not properly constructed or written.

Students do a lot of work generating other possibilities. This skill is important because it requires considering constraints. The evidence in the item provides students with information about the limits of possibilities.

Within the framework of information provided by the item, students can be very creative and can generate some wild possibilities. Stepping outside the constraints of the item, however, is not acceptable. (Note that this format precisely follows "problem-solving" situations in real life. Alternatives are possible, but only within the confines of the facts or limitations that are provided: If we don't have unlimited money, we can't consider all possibilities for rebuilding the community center.)

Using Criteria to Make Decisions.
Starting with lesson 3, students apply various criteria or requirements for making a decision. Here's the item from lesson 5.

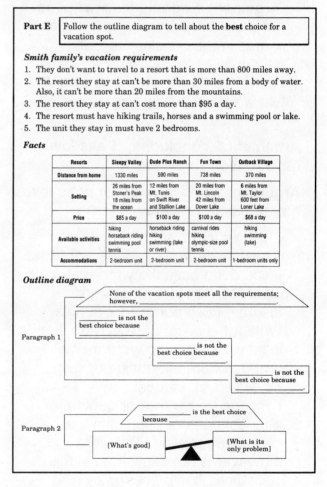

Teaching Notes

The outline diagram shows two paragraphs. The first summarizes by telling which of the examples best meets the Smith family's requirements. This paragraph points out why the other possibilities are ruled out. The second paragraph indicates why the house the student selected is the most reasonable choice.

This writing activity may require at least 15 minutes.

Expect some students to have trouble keeping track of the various requirements.

- (Write on the board:)

Sleepy Valley	Dude Plus	Fun Town	Outback

- Here's one way to figure out the problems. Take each of the requirements and write the number of that requirement next to any vacation spot that doesn't meet the requirement.
- Write 1 below any spot that is more than 800 miles away. That shows which places are ruled out by requirement 1. Then write 2 below any place that is more than 30 miles from the water and 20 miles from the mountains. When you're done, you should have a chart that shows why each of the spots fails to meet all the requirements.
- (Write to show:)

Sleepy Valley	Dude Plus	Fun Town	Outback
1, 2	3	2, 3, 4	4, 5

If students use wordy descriptions of why different resorts are ruled out, show them more concise ways of expressing the problem: **Sleepy Valley is not the best choice because it's much too far away and it is more than 20 miles from any mountain.** Or: **Sleepy Valley is not the best choice because it is 500 miles farther away than the Smith family wants to go, and it's too far from the mountains.** Make sure that students capitalize the names of these places.

If students write ragged paragraphs, direct them to write or rewrite awkward parts or parts that are missing, and then rewrite the passage.

When students read acceptable passages, point out good sentences and good ideas: "Read that first paragraph again. That was excellent wording."

Warn students that the summary for the second paragraph is supposed to be general: "Don't indicate the details that you'll spell out in the rest of the paragraph. Tell the reader in a general way why Dude Plus is the best choice."

When you check the students' work, make sure you model good summary sentences. Here are some good sentences:

Dude Plus is the best choice because it comes closest to meeting all the requirements.

Or: **Dude Plus is the best choice because it meets almost all the requirements.**

Or: **Dude Plus is the best choice because it meets all but one of the requirements.**

Or: **Dude Plus is the best choice because it meets more requirements than the others and it just misses meeting all the requirements.**

More General Conclusions. Another basic outline diagram deals with conclusions that are more general than the evidence. Here's the form of the outline diagram that is presented in lesson 6 and in lesson 7.

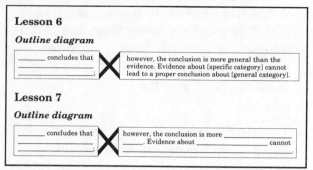

Note that in lesson 7, students are to generate the missing wording. Tell them, "Don't look at lesson 6. Just think about what the wording has to say and write it."

These are the arguments students evaluate in lesson 6.

Argument 1: Dan loves the smell of roses.
Roses are flowers with thorns.
Therefore, Dan loves the smell of all flowers with thorns.

Argument 2: Rita hates rats.
Rats are rodents.
Therefore, Rita must hate all rodents.

Argument 3: Jane Carter is an excellent fisherman.
Jane Carter is a resident of Homer Island.
Therefore, all the residents of Homer Island are excellent fishermen.

Teaching Notes

Expect some students to have problems generating the names for the specific category and the more general category.

Students may have trouble identifying the evidence that is referred to in the outline diagram. Tell them, "Read the conclusion and find the evidence that is most parallel to the conclusion. That evidence either starts out the same way the conclusion starts out or it ends the same way the conclusion ends. That's the evidence you'll refer to when you write about the argument."

Here's acceptable wording for argument 1:

. . . however, the conclusion is more general than the evidence. Evidence about the smell of roses cannot lead to a proper conclusion about the smell of all flowers with thorns.
Or:
. . . Evidence about Dan loving the smell of roses cannot lead to a proper conclusion about Dan loving the smell of all flowers with thorns.
Or:
. . . Evidence about roses cannot lead to a proper conclusion about all flowers with thorns.

Acceptable wording for argument 2:

. . . Evidence about rats cannot lead to a proper conclusion about all rodents.
Or:
. . . Evidence about Rita hating rats cannot lead to a proper conclusion about Rita hating rodents.

For argument 3:

. . . Evidence about Jane Carter cannot lead to a proper conclusion about all residents of Homer Island.
Or:
. . . Evidence about how well Jane Carter fishes cannot lead to a proper conclusion about how well all residents of Homer Island fish.

AMBIGUOUS (SILLY) MEANINGS
Throughout Level F, students write about discriminations and judgements that they make. An example is the ambiguous sentence of the type introduced in lesson 14:

The mouse ate more than the cat.

The unintended meaning of the sentence is that the mouse ate the cat and then ate some more. Instead of merely correcting the sentence, students describe the silly meaning conveyed by the sentence and indicate what a clear sentence would say. Here's the outline diagram and the items from lesson 14.

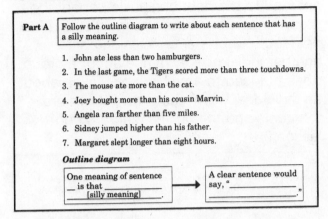

Part A | Follow the outline diagram to write about each sentence that has a silly meaning.

1. John ate less than two hamburgers.
2. In the last game, the Tigers scored more than three touchdowns.
3. The mouse ate more than the cat.
4. Joey bought more than his cousin Marvin.
5. Angela ran farther than five miles.
6. Sidney jumped higher than his father.
7. Margaret slept longer than eight hours.

Outline diagram

One meaning of sentence __ is that __ [silly meaning] . → A clear sentence would say, "_____."

Teaching Notes

Acceptable first sentences clearly identify the silly meaning.

One meaning of sentence 3 is that the mouse ate the cat.
Or:
One meaning of sentence 3 is that the mouse ate the cat and ate more.

This sentence is not acceptable: **One meaning of sentence 3 is that the mouse ate more than the cat.** If students write this sentence, point out: "That's the original sentence. You have to tell why it is silly."

Students may have trouble with some of the items. Acceptable wording for item 6 describes the height that Sidney jumped:

One meaning of sentence 6 is that Sidney jumped higher than his father's height.
Or:
One meaning of sentence 6 is that Sidney jumped high enough to go over his father.

UNCLEAR DIRECTIONS

Starting in lesson 41, students identify problems with directions that are unclear. The test of clarity is the same as that for descriptions. If one follows the directions and is able to go to more than one place, the directions are not sufficiently clear. Often they are not clear enough because they are not specific enough.

In lesson 41, students critique directions that lead to more than one house. Here's the student material from lesson 41.

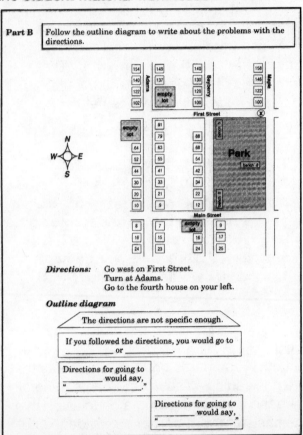

Part B | Follow the outline diagram to write about the problems with the directions.

Directions: Go west on First Street.
Turn at Adams.
Go to the fourth house on your left.

Outline diagram

The directions are not specific enough.

If you followed the directions, you would go to _____ or _____.

Directions for going to _____ would say, "_____."

Directions for going to _____ would say, "_____."

The outline diagram does not assume that we know which house the person is supposed to go to, and it provides directions for going to either house. This argument form is very powerful. It's another example of expressing possibilities. It is like the outline diagrams that start with "If . . ." and that describe different possibilities. What students are doing when they follow these diagrams is using hypotheticals that apply to very concrete situations.

Teaching Notes

For their last two sentences, students are to write about the part of the directions that would change. Sometimes, students have trouble identifying this part. They have written the sentence that tells the two places they would go to if they followed the directions. So you can help them identify the part of the directions they should refer to in their last sentences by asking them, "Why do the directions lead to 55 Adams or 154 Adams? What's missing from those directions?" (whether you turn left or right) "That's the part of the directions you write about for your last two sentences."

Here's an acceptable paragraph:

The directions are not specific enough. If you followed the directions, you would go to 55 Adams or 154 Adams. Directions for going to 55 Adams would say, "Turn left at Adams." Directions for going to 154 Adams would say, "Turn right at Adams."

MISLEADING INFORMATION

In Level F, students critique arguments that are misleading. These arguments generally take the form of drawing a conclusion that is consistent with part of the evidence but ignoring important evidence. These arguments are often used to promote practices or people by focusing on their virtue. Sometimes they involve techniques that are invalid, like confusing the individual with the group. Some arguments make numbers lie by using inappropriate statistical techniques or reporting about the numbers in a way that distorts the facts.

Individual-Group Fallacies. In lesson 26, students are introduced to misleading arguments that involve individuals who are in groups. Students apply these basic rules: Evidence about an individual does not lead to a proper conclusion about the group; evidence about one individual does not lead to a proper conclusion about another individual; evidence about a group does not lead to a proper conclusion about an individual within the group. Here are the items and the outline diagram from lesson 26.

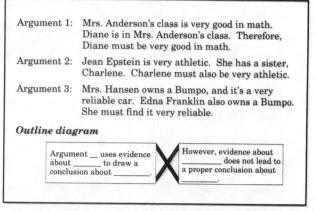

Here are adequate paragraphs that explain the problems with the three arguments:

Argument 1 uses evidence about Mrs. Anderson's class to draw a conclusion about Diane. However, evidence about a group does not lead to a proper conclusion about an individual within the group.

Argument 2 uses evidence about Jean to draw a conclusion about Charlene. However, evidence about an individual does not lead to a proper conclusion about another individual.

Argument 3 uses evidence about Mrs. Hansen's Bumpo to draw a conclusion about Edna Franklin's Bumpo. However, evidence about an individual does not lead to a proper conclusion about another individual.

The outline diagram prescribes the wording in a tight format. In later lessons, however, students are expected to generate this wording. Here is an example of independent work from lesson 29:

Part E	Write about the problems with each argument. Use the appropriate outline diagram.
	Argument 1: Eddie Nelson is one of the best workers I have ever seen. I'll bet the entire Nelson family is a hardworking family.
	Argument 2: I went to Vern's Restaurant and had a chicken sandwich that was not very good. I'll bet Vern's pizza is as bad as the chicken sandwich.
	Argument 3: Brandon High has the worst football team in the city. Denny plays on that team. He must be a terrible player.

All three arguments draw inappropriate conclusions. Students are required to generate the appropriate wording to explain the problems.

Part-Whole Fallacies. In lesson 61, students expand the concept of group and individual to whole and part. The rules that they learn parallel those for individuals in groups. You can't draw a proper conclusion about a whole from evidence about a part; you can't draw a proper conclusion about a part from evidence about a whole; you can't draw a proper conclusion about a part from evidence about another part.

The outline diagram is similar to that for groups and individuals.

Argument 1: The car has the finest heater made. Therefore, the car must be a superior car.

Argument 2: Dr. Brown and Dr. Dennis have offices in the Ferris Building. Dr. Brown's office is very cold every time I'm in it. Therefore, Dr. Dennis's office must also be very cold.

Argument 3: I have seen beautiful banana trees in North Cove on Diller Island. The whole island must be covered with banana trees.

Outline diagram

Argument __ uses evidence about _____ to draw a conclusion about _____.	However, evidence about _____ does not lead to a proper conclusion about _____.

The practice with the wording required for this outline diagram provides students with greater flexibility in expressing the relationships.

Misleading Statistics. Students receive practice in identifying parts and wholes in arguments. In lesson 66, they are introduced to a variation of misleading arguments that involve parts and wholes. These arguments involve statistics. Statistics do nothing more than measure individuals and draw conclusions about the whole. Statistics can be used in any of the part-whole fallacies. Arguments based on statistics draw misleading conclusions by using numbers to confuse parts and wholes, to draw evidence about the whole that is based on information about nonrepresentative individuals, or to use words like "double" or "increase by 60 percent" to describe relatively small gains. Here's part of the introduction from lesson 66.

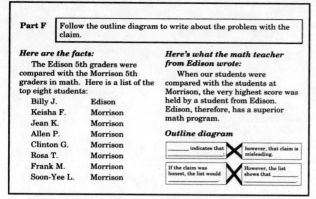

Part F — Follow the outline diagram to write about the problem with the claim.

Here are the facts:

The Edison 5th graders were compared with the Morrison 5th graders in math. Here is a list of the top eight students:

Billy J.	Edison
Keisha F.	Morrison
Jean K.	Morrison
Allen P.	Morrison
Clinton G.	Morrison
Rosa T.	Morrison
Frank M.	Morrison
Soon-Yee L.	Morrison

Here's what the math teacher from Edison wrote:

When our students were compared with the students at Morrison, the very highest score was held by a student from Edison. Edison, therefore, has a superior math program.

Outline diagram

3. You're going to write about the problem with the math teacher's claim.

- You'll tell that it is misleading and why it is misleading. To do that, you'll indicate what the list of top students would show if the claim were honest compared to what it does show.

- If it were true that Edison has a superior math program, what would the list of top students show? (Call on a student. Idea: *Most of them would be from Edison.*)

4. The outline diagram shows two pairs of X boxes.

5. Write your sentence for the first pair of X boxes. Indicate the part of the math teacher's claim that is misleading and indicate that it is misleading. Pencils down when you've done your first pair of X boxes.

(Observe students and give feedback.)

- Here is a good sentence:
The math teacher from Edison indicates that Edison has a superior math program; however, that claim is misleading.

- (Call on several students to read their sentence. Praise good sentences that follow the outline diagram.)

6. Now write your sentences for the second pair of X boxes. Indicate what the list of top students would show and what the list actually shows. Be specific. Give enough information to make it clear that the teacher's claim is misleading. Pencils down when you're finished.

(Observe students and give feedback.)

- Here are good sentences for the second pair of X boxes:
If the claim was honest, the list would show that most of the top students are from Edison. However, the list shows that only one of the top eight students is from Edison.

- (Call on several students to read their sentences. Correct sentences that do not provide sufficient information to explain the problem.)

Teaching Notes

In step 6, students do the hard part of the assignment. They indicate what the list of top students would show if the claim was honest. Students may be too specific. Remind them: "Give the reader a picture of any list that is honest. Tell what it shows."

When you call on students to read their sentence, praise sentences that describe a good list. This sentence is too specific:

If the claim was honest, the list would show six of the top students from Edison and two of the top students from Morrison.

Respond to sentences like that by asking, "Is that the only list that would be honest? You want to be a little more general. You could say that it would have at least five of the top students from Edison."

Students work on similar exercises to the end of the program. They continue to apply the strategy of indicating what the evidence would show to support the conclusion and what the evidence actually shows. Some of the arguments students critique use words like "more" to draw misleading conclusions. Here's the exercise from lesson 67.

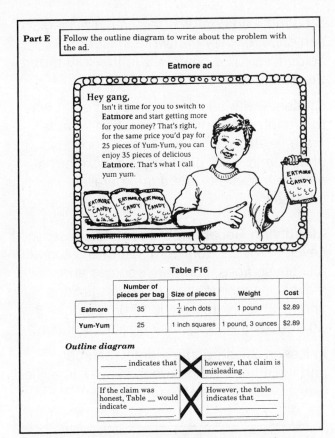

Part E — Follow the outline diagram to write about the problem with the ad.

Eatmore ad

Hey gang,
Isn't it time for you to switch to **Eatmore** and start getting more for your money? That's right, for the same price you'd pay for 25 pieces of Yum-Yum, you can enjoy 35 pieces of delicious **Eatmore**. That's what I call yum yum.

Table F16

	Number of pieces per bag	Size of pieces	Weight	Cost
Eatmore	35	$\frac{1}{4}$ inch dots	1 pound	$2.89
Yum-Yum	25	1 inch squares	1 pound, 3 ounces	$2.89

Outline diagram

_____ indicates that _____; however, that claim is misleading.

If the claim was honest, Table __ would indicate _____. However, the table indicates that _____.

To find the flaw in the arguments, students refer to the table: A bag of Eatmore weighs three ounces less than a bag of Yum-Yum. Therefore, the conclusion that Eatmore gives more for the money is misleading. It gives more pieces of candy for the money, not more total candy. By following the outline diagram, students are able to describe this distinction by pointing out what the "evidence" would be if the claim was honest:

If the claim was honest, Table F16 would indicate that a bag of Eatmore weighs more than a bag of Yum-Yum. However, the table indicates that a bag of Eatmore weighs three ounces less than a bag of Yum-Yum.

In lesson 69, students critique an argument that compares samples that are not comparable. The conclusion the argument draws, however, assumes that the samples are comparable.

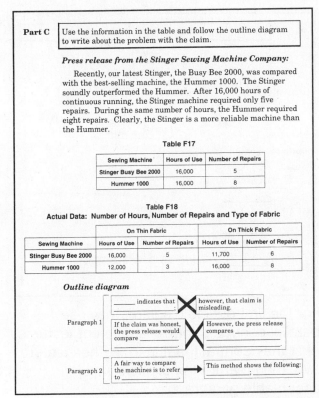

Part C — Use the information in the table and follow the outline diagram to write about the problem with the claim.

Press release from the Stinger Sewing Machine Company:

Recently, our latest Stinger, the Busy Bee 2000, was compared with the best-selling machine, the Hummer 1000. The Stinger soundly outperformed the Hummer. After 16,000 hours of continuous running, the Stinger machine required only five repairs. During the same number of hours, the Hummer required eight repairs. Clearly, the Stinger is a more reliable machine than the Hummer.

Table F17

Sewing Machine	Hours of Use	Number of Repairs
Stinger Busy Bee 2000	16,000	5
Hummer 1000	16,000	8

Table F18
Actual Data: Number of Hours, Number of Repairs and Type of Fabric

Sewing Machine	On Thin Fabric		On Thick Fabric	
	Hours of Use	Number of Repairs	Hours of Use	Number of Repairs
Stinger Busy Bee 2000	16,000	5	11,700	6
Hummer 1000	12,000	3	16,000	8

Outline diagram

Paragraph 1

_____ indicates that _____. however, that claim is misleading.

If the claim was honest, the press release would compare _____. However, the press release compares _____.

Paragraph 2

A fair way to compare the machines is to refer to _____. This method shows the following: _____; _____.

This activity requires more writing time than earlier assignments. In addition to pointing out what the evidence would show, students describe a fair comparison (paragraph 2). They refer to something that is like miles per gallon: hours between repairs. This method shows the following: On thin fabric, Hummer goes 800 hours longer than Stinger before needing repairs; on thick fabric, Hummer goes 50 hours longer before needing repairs. The exercise leads students through the computation and the development of the test.

COMPARING AND SYNTHESIZING INFORMATION
Compare and Contrast. In lesson 16, students write about the same information two ways, using two different forms of parallel comparisons. Here is the exercise and the outline diagram from lesson 16.

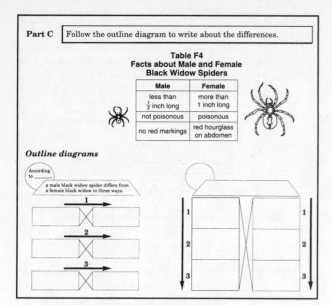

Part C | Follow the outline diagram to write about the differences.

Table F4
Facts about Male and Female
Black Widow Spiders

Male	Female
less than $\frac{1}{2}$ inch long	more than 1 inch long
not poisonous	poisonous
no red markings	red hourglass on abdomen

Outline diagrams

For the first outline diagram, they use parallel contrasts for three different features. First they contrast feature one, then feature two, then feature three. Here's an acceptable paragraph:

According to Table F4, a male black widow spider differs from a female black widow in three ways. The male is less than one-half inch long, but the female is more than an inch long. The male is not poisonous, but the female is. The male has no red markings, but the female has a red hourglass on her abdomen.

For the other paragraph, students list the three features of the male black widow and then the corresponding three features of the female. Here's an acceptable paragraph:

According to Table F4, a male black widow spider differs from a female black widow in three ways. The male is less than one-half inch long. The male is not poisonous, and he has no red markings. The female is over an inch long. She is poisonous, and she has a red hourglass on her abdomen.

Students can combine features in a single sentence, or they can write separate sentences. The point is that they organize the information so it is parallel.

Students with a knowledge of different ways to organize the same information have far more flexibility in their writing. They also understand what both organization forms have in common—the same parallel contrasts.

Identifying Reliable Sources. Exercises in Level F provide work with sources. Students identify sources, compare sources and identify inconsistencies or contradictions, and synthesize information from sources that do not cover exactly the same information.

In lesson 37, students identify sources and indicate which sources answer specific questions. Here's an example from lesson 37.

Part A | Write **Part A** in the left margin of your paper and number it from 1 to 12. Read the passage and study the table below. Then write the answers to the questions.

Passage

On Monday morning, Ms. Hassel returned English and math tests to her class and explained her grading system.

Here's a summary: One hundred points were possible.

Fifty points were possible on the math test.

Fifty points were possible on the English test.

A student had to earn at least 30 points to pass each part.

A student needed a total score of 70 points to pass the test.

Two students did not pass the English test.

All students passed the math test.

The hardest part was the editing part of the English test. Many students left words misspelled, and the students were weak on placing commas appropriately.

Students who did well all year on the homework assignments did well on the tests.

Two students who did little or no homework also did well on the tests.

The two students who scored less than 30 on the English test will spend some extra time with the teacher this week. They will take the test again on Friday.

Student	Math	English	Total	Absent
1. Alvin	36	48	84	
2. Owen	42	29	71	
3. Kim	50	35	85	
4. Frank				x
5. Sharon	46	45	91	
6. Rainbow	41	39	80	
7. Tofu	37	33	70	
8. Henry	49	47	96	
9. Joseph	33	24	57	
10. Brian	46	42	88	
11. Cecily				x
12. Marilyn	44	41	85	
13. Laurie	48	45	93	
14. James	50	49	99	
15. Peter	41	43	84	
16. Martha	39	37	76	
17. Nancy	43	39	82	
18. David	46	41	87	
19. Leroy	37	39	76	
20. Candice	41	42	83	
21. Mary	50	49	99	
22. Nickolas	48	42	90	
23. Mick	39	34	73	
24. Tina	49	38	77	
25. Regina	45	40	75	

The item consists of a passage and a table. Students are provided with a list of questions. Some of them are answered by the passage, some by the table, and some by both.

Questions are like this:

How many points are possible on the entire test? (answered by passage)

Did more students pass the English test or the math test? (answered by passage and table)

How many students were absent? (answered by table)

In lesson 45, students indicate which sources are appropriate to answer different questions. They write the answer by referring to the source. Here's the student work from lesson 45.

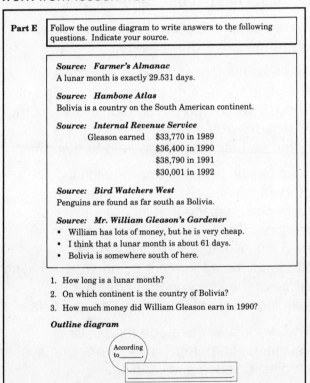

To answer question 1, students follow the outline diagram and write, **According to the Farmer's Almanac, the lunar month is 29.531 days.**

In lesson 46, students identify a contradiction in two accounts:

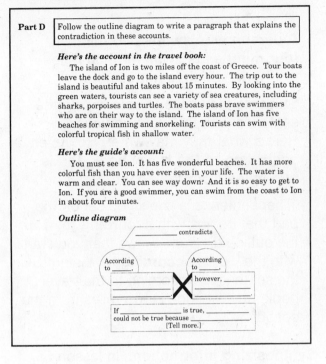

Teaching Notes

Here's an acceptable paragraph:

The guide's account contradicts the travel book. According to the guide's account, a good swimmer can swim from the coast to Ion in about four minutes. According to the travel book, however, Ion is two miles from the coast. If the travel book account is true, the guide's account cannot be true because no person could swim two miles in four minutes. Nobody could even run two miles in four minutes.

The last sentence could say something like this:

A person who swims two miles in four minutes is swimming 30 miles per hour, which is impossible.

Students may have trouble writing the sentence with the word **however.** Here's what they may write: **However, according to the travel book, Ion is two miles from the coast.** Point out:

"That sentence is fine if you set off the part that begins with **according to.** But the outline diagram shows that you start with the words **according to.** Listen to the sentence: According to the travel book, however, Ion is two miles from the coast."

Synthesizing Information. In lesson 55, students identify a contradiction and synthesize the information from two accounts. Here's the item and outline diagram from lesson 55.

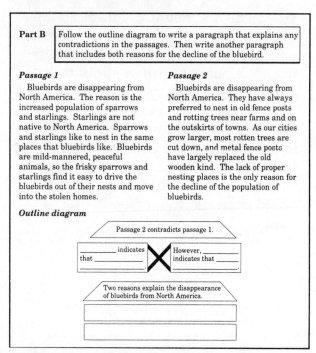

Part B | Follow the outline diagram to write a paragraph that explains any contradictions in the passages. Then write another paragraph that includes both reasons for the decline of the bluebird.

Passage 1

Bluebirds are disappearing from North America. The reason is the increased population of sparrows and starlings. Starlings are not native to North America. Sparrows and starlings like to nest in the same places that bluebirds like. Bluebirds are mild-mannered, peaceful animals, so the frisky sparrows and starlings find it easy to drive the bluebirds out of their nests and move into the stolen homes.

Passage 2

Bluebirds are disappearing from North America. They have always preferred to nest in old fence posts and rotting trees near farms and on the outskirts of towns. As our cities grow larger, most rotten trees are cut down, and metal fence posts have largely replaced the old wooden kind. The lack of proper nesting places is the only reason for the decline of the population of bluebirds.

Outline diagram

To write about the argument, students must summarize the key assertions.

For their X-box sentences, students may describe the contradiction in different ways:

Passage 1 indicates that sparrows and starlings drive bluebirds out of their nests.

Passage 1 indicates that the increased population of sparrows and starlings took over the bluebirds' nesting places.

Passage 1 indicates that the bluebirds are disappearing from North America because of the increased population of sparrows and starlings.

Students may write bad sentences that try to express this cause:

Passage 1 indicates that the increased population of sparrows and starlings is the reason.

Passage 1 indicates that sparrows and starlings nest in the same places.

Passage 1 indicates that sparrows and starlings drive them away.

All these sentences lack specific detail. Respond to them by saying, "You didn't give enough information. You didn't mention the bluebirds. You have to mention them by name and tell what happened to them."

After writing about the contradiction, students synthesize the passages. They write one passage that incorporates both reasons. This passage is to be no longer than either of the original passages. Students must therefore summarize, omitting some of the less important detail, but keeping enough to make the account clear.

This work sets the stage for similar assignments, particularly in work with social studies, science and reading.

Similes. Similes are an extension of the work that students do with parallelism. Similes are based on **parallel meanings.** The simile presents two things that are the same to the extent you can make parallel true statements about them. If a sunburned person is like a baked potato, it should be possible to make parallel true statements about a sunburned person and a baked potato.

Students are introduced to similes in lesson 51. They write a sentence that refers to both things named in a simile. They first identify the pronoun that refers to both things. Then they write a sentence that starts with that pronoun and that is true about either thing named in the simile. Here's part of the introduction from lesson 51.

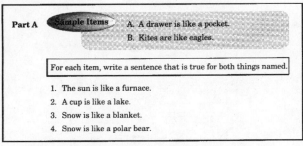

Part A   Sample Items   A. A drawer is like a pocket.
                          B. Kites are like eagles.

For each item, write a sentence that is true for both things named.

1. The sun is like a furnace.
2. A cup is like a lake.
3. Snow is like a blanket.
4. Snow is like a polar bear.

4. Item 1: **The sun is like a furnace.**
• What's the pronoun that applies to either the **sun** or a **furnace?** (Signal.) *It.*
• Write the sentence that starts with **it** and that could tell about either the **sun** or a **furnace.** Pencils down when you're finished.

(Observe students and give feedback.)
• Here's a good sentence:
‖ It gives off heat.
• (Call on several students to read their sentence. Test each sentence by asking: **Does it start with the right pronoun? Could the sentence be used to tell about either the sun or a furnace?**)

5. Item 2: **A cup is like a lake.**
• Write the sentence. Pencils down when you're finished.

(Observe students and give feedback.)
• Here's a good sentence:
‖ It holds water.
• (Call on several students to read their sentence. Test each sentence by asking: **Does it start with the right pronoun? Could the sentence be used to tell about either a cup or a lake?**)

6. Item 3: **Snow is like a blanket.**
• Write the sentence. Make sure your sentence tells about either thing named. Pencils down when you're finished.

(Observe students and give feedback.)
• Here's a good sentence:
‖ It covers things.
• (Call on several students to read their sentence. Test each sentence by asking: **Does it start with the right pronoun? Could the sentence be used to tell about either the snow or a blanket?**)

Teaching Notes

Some students may not identify the right pronoun. Specifically, they identify the pronoun for a cup or a lake as **they.**

"Say the word that replaces **a cup.**" (Signal.) *It.*

"Say the word that replaces **a lake.**" (Signal.) *It.*

"Say the word that replaces either **a cup** or **a lake.**" (Signal.) *It.*

This test applies to items that have plurals such as: **Kites are like eagles.**

"Say the pronoun that replaces **kites.**" (Signal.) *They.*

"Say the pronoun that replaces **eagles.**" (Signal.) *They.*

"Say the pronoun that replaces either **kites** or **eagles.**" (Signal.) *They.*

Also use the other tests that are indicated for evaluating sentences that students read to the group. Ask the group:

"Does that sentence start with the right pronoun?"

"Could that sentence be used to tell about either a cup or a lake?"

If the answer to either question is no, direct students to fix up what they wrote.

Analogies. In lesson 53, students work with parallel opposites:

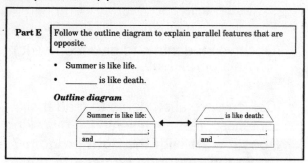

Students write sentences that tell about life. They follow the same sequence to write parallel features about death. Here's an acceptable paragraph:

Summer is like life: The days are warm; the sun is hot; and plants are green. Winter is like death: The days are cold; the sun is cool; and plants are brown.

Teaching Notes

Point out: "The more parallel your sentences are, the better your writing is." Help students make sentences more parallel, even colorful:

In summer, waters move freely and the shadows are warm. In winter, waters are frozen and the shadows are cold.

Extended analogies are introduced in lesson 56. Students work with aphorisms like: **Saving money is like growing a vegetable garden.** They write pairs of parallel sentences that tell about the various similarities.

Here's the exercise from lesson 56.

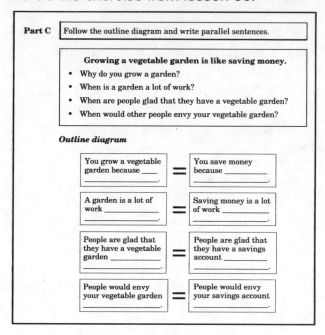

RULE GENERATING, RULE TESTING AND CONSISTENCY

Rule Testing. In lesson 9, students express how they would test the validity of a rule. They tell how many subjects they would examine and what type of subjects they would examine. Then they explain the observations that would discredit the rule and the observations that would not. Here's the item and the outline diagram from lesson 9.

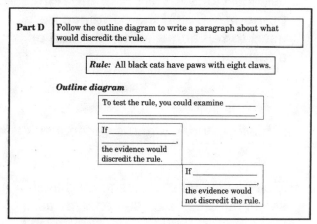

Teaching Notes

Usage: The models that students follow do not use the subjunctive mood. The reasons are:

1) the outcomes are possible and therefore, non-subjunctive verbs are acceptable, if not preferable;
2) subjunctive verbs are used less than they have been in the past;
3) the rules for using the subjunctive complicate the use of regular verbs and of noun-verb agreement (if I **were** . . .).

If students use the subjunctive appropriately, don't require them to change. Point out that what they write is perfectly acceptable. However, don't require other students to use it.

Content of writing: This exercise, like many others in the program, requires students to make a judgement about the number and type of subjects they will test. The number is based on judgements about 1) their knowledge of the things that are governed by the rule; 2) the range of variation that the rule addresses; 3) whether the rule tells about a group or about individuals.

2 and 3 deal with the same issue. If there's a great range of variation in the sample that is tested (the Tiger football team eats more than the Jets football team eats), a lot of observations are implied. On the other extreme, for a rule about whether all cats have eight claws, the student who has a suspicion that the rule is wrong knows that only one cat that doesn't have eight claws will discredit the rule, and the student would specify testing possibly only three to five cats. If the student did not know how many claws cats have and suspected that the rule might be true,

the student would need to test a larger number of cats, possibly 12 or more. (If the rule was true, the student would need enough to show that enough cats were tested to imply that the rule would hold for a larger sample.)

Here's a good way to guide students in selecting numbers for rules about individuals. Ask, "Do you believe that the rule is true or that there's a good possibility that it might be true? If the answer is yes, you need to test quite a few cases. If the answer is no, you don't have to test as many cases."

In lesson 14, students write about testing rules that are completely unfamiliar. Here are the items from lesson 14.

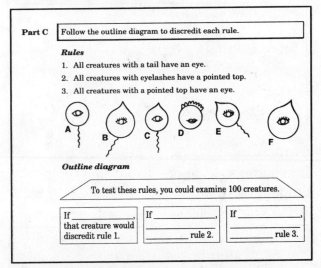

The outline diagram suggests that you examine a large number of cases. The reason is that the population has a lot of variation. Although the rules hold for the sample that is shown, each individual could vary in a number of ways: round versus pointed head; hair versus none; eye versus none; lips versus none; eyelashes versus none; and tail versus none.

Revising Rules Based on New Evidence.

In lesson 17, students write rules based on a small sample of strange pets.

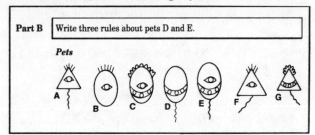

| Part B | Write three rules about pets D and E. |

Pets

They write these rules about pets D and E:

1. **All bald pets have a round head.**
2. **All bald pets have a collar.**
3. **All bald pets have a tail.**

Students then examine a larger sample of bald pets.

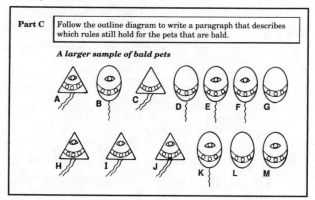

| Part C | Follow the outline diagram to write a paragraph that describes which rules still hold for the pets that are bald. |

A larger sample of bald pets

This sample discredits two of the rules. Students follow the outline diagram to write about the specifics.

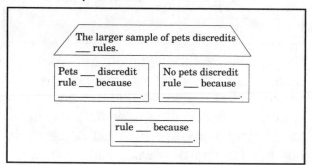

Teaching Notes

Here's an acceptable paragraph:

The larger sample of pets discredits two rules. Pets A, C, H, I and J discredit rule 1 because all those pets are bald; however, they have a pointed head. Pets G, L and M discredit rule 3 because they are bald; however, they do not have a tail. No pets discredit rule 2 because all the bald pets in the larger sample have a collar.

Different wording is acceptable; however, the students' paragraphs must clearly indicate that the pets are bald but that they . . .

The order in which rules are discussed is also optional. Students could tell about the rules in this order—1, 2, 3 or in this order—1, 3, 2.

These sentences are not acceptable:

Pets A, C, H, I and J discredit 1 rule because they have pointed heads. (The sentence must also mention that these pets are bald.)

Pets A, C, H, I and J discredit rule 1 because they are bald. (The sentence must also mention that they have a pointed head.)

Throughout Level F, students do similar exercises. They make up rules based on a sample of examples; they indicate the features of examples that would discredit each of the rules; they later examine a larger sample and indicate which rules are discredited, which individuals discredit particular rules, and why.

Students who become facile at solving these problems and writing about them have a good understanding of what science is all about.

Noting Inconsistencies and Contradictions. Some writing exercises involve conclusions that are consistent with some of the evidence but not all of it. This argument form is very common in advertising and in promoting plans of action. The good features are used as evidence for positive conclusions. Other evidence is ignored. Here's the outline diagram and the information from lesson 21.

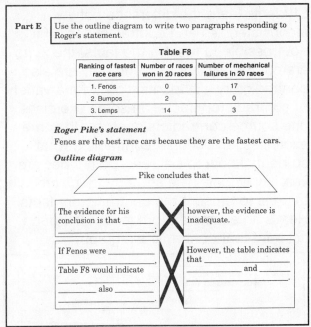

Part E Use the outline diagram to write two paragraphs responding to Roger's statement.

Table F8

Ranking of fastest race cars	Number of races won in 20 races	Number of mechanical failures in 20 races
1. Fenos	0	17
2. Bumpos	2	0
3. Lemps	14	3

Roger Pike's statement
Fenos are the best race cars because they are the fastest cars.

Outline diagram

_____ Pike concludes that _____ .

The evidence for his conclusion is that _____ ; however, the evidence is inadequate.

If Fenos were _____ , Table F8 would indicate _____ also _____ However, the table indicates that _____ and _____

Teaching Notes

Students apply what they have learned about consistency. If Pike's conclusion about Fenos was consistent with the facts, the facts would be different. They would show that Fenos are mechanically sound and that they do not have mechanical failures. They would also indicate that Fenos win races.

The sentences that students write take the form: If (it were true that) . . . other things would be different from what the facts show. The facts actually show that . . . So the conclusion is unreasonable.

This argument form is very powerful, By assuming that the conclusion is true, the form is able to show what would have to be different.

In later lessons, students work with this same form in different outline-diagram contexts. In lesson 32, for example, students identify the inconsistency in a pattern. Here's the table and the outline diagram from that lesson.

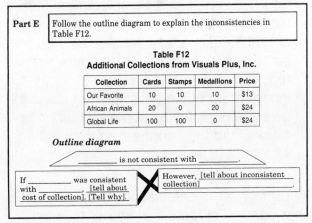

Part E Follow the outline diagram to explain the inconsistencies in Table F12.

Table F12
Additional Collections from Visuals Plus, Inc.

Collection	Cards	Stamps	Medallions	Price
Our Favorite	10	10	10	$13
African Animals	20	0	20	$24
Global Life	100	100	0	$24

Outline diagram

_____ is not consistent with _____ .

If _____ was consistent with _____ , [tell about cost of collection]. [Tell why]. However, [tell about inconsistent collection]

In the preceding lesson, students had figured out that each card cost 20 cents; each stamp cost 10 cents; and each medallion cost 1 dollar. (They completed a table that had consistent pricing for different collections.) They apply the same pricing to the collections presented in lesson 32 and write about the collection that is not priced consistently.

Another type of exercise involves passages that contradict facts that students know or facts they receive. Students learn (lesson 25) that things are inconsistent if they don't agree with what they expect. Things are consistent if they do agree with what they expect.

Students do exercises with apparent inconsistencies. They make up facts that resolve the inconsistencies. For example, Mrs. Anderson loves plants. She has worked in a florist shop. She has a large backyard. However, she has a very tiny garden, not the large garden we might expect. Students make up a fact that resolves the apparent inconsistency. (She has arthritis. She is not in good health, etc.)

Students learn the difference between inconsistencies and contradictions. If it is not possible to resolve the facts, the facts are not merely inconsistent; they are also contradictory. Students work with a variety of contradictory facts. In some exercises, one source contradicts another. In some exercises, an account contradicts what students know to be true. Both types are very important. The strategy for discrediting them is to present the contradictory facts. Here's an example, from lesson 41, of an account that contradicts a graph.

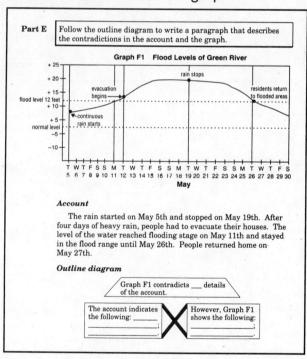

The outline diagram requires the students to make a parallel list.

Teaching Notes

The punctuation involves colons and semicolons. Here's an acceptable paragraph:

Graph F1 contradicts two details of the account. The account indicates the following: People evacuated their houses after four days of heavy rain; and people returned home on May 27. However, Graph F1 shows the following: People evacuated their houses after seven days of heavy rain; and people returned home on May 26.

Note that the outline diagram is perfectly arbitrary. Students could write about the same information different ways. By following this particular diagram, however, students get practice in writing parallel lists. In this case, the lists are sentences. The form that is used applies to a lot of writing situations. Make sure that students follow the wording and punctuation requirements precisely. Also make sure that they have parallel sentences and sentences in the same order for the two sources of information.

In this exercise and similar ones, students don't know which source of information is accurate. They know only that the sources contradict each other on details.

In lesson 44, students are introduced to contradictions of a different type. Passages present information that contradicts what students know. Here's an example from lesson 44.

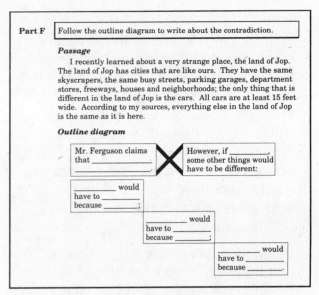

Part F — Follow the outline diagram to write about the contradiction.

Passage

I recently learned about a very strange place, the land of Jop. The land of Jop has cities that are like ours. They have the same skyscrapers, the same busy streets, parking garages, department stores, freeways, houses and neighborhoods; the only thing that is different in the land of Jop is the cars. All cars are at least 15 feet wide. According to my sources, everything else in the land of Jop is the same as it is here.

Outline diagram

Students have to identify three contradictions. Those are three things that would have to be different if the only difference in the land of Jop was that cars were at least 15 feet wide.

Teaching Notes

Here's an acceptable paragraph:

Mr. Ferguson claims that the only thing that is different in the land of Jop is the width of cars. However, if the cars were 15 feet wide, some other things would have to be different: Garages would have to be wider and have wider doors because a car 15 feet wide couldn't fit through an ordinary garage door; parking garages would have to be much larger because regular parking garages couldn't hold enough cars; streets would have to be wider because parked cars would take up a lot of space.

Students may have several problems. The first is that they are unable to generate contradictions. Tell them to assume that everything in the passage is true and then to think about doing various things in one of those wide cars. Some students may have trouble with this idea. Tell them: "Just pretend that you have a car that is 15 feet wide. What are some of the things you do with a car? Where do you take it? What do you do with it when you are not driving? In each of those situations, would something have to change if all cars were 15 feet wide? Would the doorway have to change?"

When students read their paragraph, test the various contradictions by saying, "Would the thing you identify **have to** change if cars were 15 feet wide?" (Students might say that narrow streets would have to change because there couldn't be parked cars.) Ask, "Would the streets have to change or would it be possible to keep the streets we have now?"

Lead students to the conclusion that some streets would definitely have to change (maybe becoming one-way streets). For other streets, parking regulations would have to change. (In either case, something would have to change.)

Designing Experiments. Another version of rule testing occurs in lesson 58. Students are provided with a scenario, a conclusion and a list of other possibilities that are consistent with evidence in the conclusion. Students indicate how they would test the other possibilities. By ruling out each of those possibilities, the original possibility would be the only one that could apply. (This form of argument is important for dealing with possibilities. It's not possible to fully test the most probable; however, it's possible to test alternatives and show that they are not valid. Therefore, in the absence of competition explanations, the probable one is accepted.) Here's the exercise from lesson 58.

Part C | Read the passage and the possibilities. Follow the outline diagram to describe how Joe could test each possibility.

Passage

Joe had a girlfriend who was happy sometimes and unhappy at other times. Joe thought about her moods and figured out this rule: **When I give somebody else a present, she feels bad. When I give her a present, she feels wonderful.**

As Joe thought about this rule and about the evidence that he had to support the rule, he decided that there were other possible rules that could explain the way his girlfriend behaved. Maybe she just happened to like the two things he gave her—shoelaces and gum. Maybe she was just grouchy on the days that he gave somebody else a present.

Joe decided that he would test the rule that he had made up. His test would have to rule out other possibilities.

Other possibilities

1. Joe's girlfriend is unhappy unless the gift she gets is shoelaces or gum.
2. Joe's girlfriend just happened to be happy on days that she received gifts from Joe.
3. Joe's girlfriend would feel sad if anybody gave presents to other people.

Outline diagram

Paragraph 1
- To test the possibility that _____.
- If _____, the test would discredit _____ that _____.
- If _____, the test would not discredit that possibility.

Paragraph 2
- To test the possibility that _____.
- If _____, the test would discredit _____ that _____.
- If _____, the test would not discredit that possibility.

Paragraph 3
- To test the possibility that _____.
- If _____, the test would discredit _____ that _____.
- If _____, the test would not discredit that possibility.

Teaching Notes

Here's an acceptable passage:

To test the possibility that the gift must be shoelaces or gum, Joe could give his girlfriend an inexpensive gift that is not shoelaces or gum. If she is happy, the test would discredit the possibility that the gift must be shoelaces or gum. If she is sad, the test would not discredit that possibility.

To test the possibility that the girlfriend just happened to be happy on the two days she received gifts, Joe could give his girlfriend shoelaces or gum on four days in a row. If she is happy every time, the test would discredit the possibility that she just happened to be happy on the two earlier days. If she is not happy every time, the test would not discredit that possibility.

To test the possibility that the girlfriend would feel sad if anybody gave presents to other people, Joe could arrange for a pal to buy things for Joe's brother and for Joe's mother. If the girlfriend does not feel sad, the test would discredit the possibility that she gets sad when anybody gives presents to other people. If his girlfriend does feel sad, the test would not discredit that possibility.

Students may make a variety of writing errors in trying to describe the test. The most common mistakes they make involve sentences that have unclear pronouns and sentences that don't have enough words to be clear. For example, students might write: **If his girlfriend is very happy, the test would discredit the possibility.** The sentence doesn't have enough words. It doesn't tell which possibility it refers to. Here's a sentence that has unclear pronouns: **If his girlfriend is very happy, the test would discredit the possibility that it just happened then.**

Correct by leading students to sentences that have sufficient information: **If his girlfriend is very happy, the test would discredit the possibility that she just happened to be happy on the days Joe had given her gifts.**

A good plan is to have a large number of students read their passage, have the class identify the problems and how the sentences could be changed, then direct all students to start with a fresh sheet of paper and, without referring to what they wrote earlier or to the corrections, follow the outline diagram and rewrite the passage. (This writing may have to be scheduled during a later period.)

False Cause. Starting in lesson 61, students write about arguments that identify a false cause. Here's part of the exercise from lesson 61.

> Argument 1: Robins are not around during cold weather. Robins are around during warm weather. The way to make the weather warmer is to keep robins around.

5. Argument 1: **Robins are not around during cold weather. Robins are around during warm weather. The way to make the weather warmer is to keep robins around.**
• You're going to follow the outline diagram and write about this argument.
6. The argument has the mistaken belief that something actually makes something else happen. Your first sentence will indicate what causes what.
• Write your summary sentence. Pencils down when you've done that much. (Observe students and give feedback.)
• (Write on the board:)

Argument 1 assumes that robins cause warm weather.

• Here's a good summary sentence: **Argument 1 assumes that robins cause warm weather.** Raise your hand if you wrote that sentence.

- You could have written:
  Argument 1 assumes that the presence of robins causes warm weather.
- Or:
  Argument 1 assumes that robins cause the weather to get warmer.
- **(Call on several students to read their sentence. Praise good sentences. Correct awkward wording or inappropriate sentences.)**

7. Now write about the evidence. Summarize the evidence. Remember, the evidence has to do with **two things that occur together.** Don't write everything that is in the original evidence. Just summarize the two things. Pencils down when you've written about the evidence.
   (Observe students and give feedback.)

- Here's a good sentence about the evidence:
  The evidence is that robins are not around when the weather is cold but are present when the weather is warm.
- Or you could have written something like this:
  The evidence is that robins and warm weather occur together.
- Or:
  The evidence is that the only time robins are around is during warm weather.
- Here is a sentence that is not good:
  Robins are around in warm weather.
  The sentence should say: **Robins are around *only* in warm weather.**
- **(Call on several students to read their sentence. Praise good sentences. Correct sentences that are awkward.)**

8. Your turn: Write the rest of the paragraph. For the last sentence, tell what somebody would have to do with robins to prove that they cause warmer weather. Be specific. You can use more than one sentence. Pencils down when you're finished.
   (Observe students and give feedback.)

- Here's a good ending to the paragraph:
  However, this evidence is inadequate. Adequate evidence would show that we took robins to 20 different places in the winter and made the weather warmer.
- Or you could write:
  Adequate evidence would show that the weather got warmer in 10 places during the winter when we brought robins to those places.
- Or:
  Adequate evidence would show that the temperature went up in 10 cities when we sent robins to the cities.
- **(Call on several students to read their entire paragraph. Praise paragraphs that follow the outline diagram and that have reasonable sentences.)**

Teaching Notes

Students may have trouble identifying the cause in step 6. If students have trouble, tell them that the thing that makes something else change is the cause. In the argument, what thing makes the change? What kind of change are robins supposed to make? If robins make the weather get warmer, robins cause the weather to get warmer.

Expect students to have some trouble identifying what adequate evidence would show. These attempts would not provide adequate evidence:

Adequate evidence would show that there are robins in warmer places and no robins in colder places.

Adequate evidence would show that every time the robins leave, the weather gets colder.

Step 8 of the exercise gives samples of adequate evidence. Tell students: "Adequate evidence would leave no doubt in your mind that robins actually make the weather change."

Projects

The major thrust of the writing activities in Level F is to provide students with both the information and flexibility they need to explain problems with statements, claims, arguments, directions or descriptions that are inaccurate, misleading or unclear.

The outline diagrams they follow change from one assignment to another. This variation promotes flexibility. At the same time, the outline diagrams refer to the same sorts of tests and the same techniques. If the conclusion of the argument was valid, the evidence would have to be different. If we accept the evidence of the argument, we could draw more than one conclusion. If the account is intended to identify one thing, it would have to say this: . . . To identify another thing, it would have to say this . . .

These techniques are powerful. They set the stage for a lot of extension activities, including those that are included in the last lessons of the program. These activities build on what students have already learned. Each team activity requires at least one full period, often more.

In lesson 71, students apply what they have learned about parallel grammatical functions to figure out which words could be conjunctions. (They are told not to use **and, but, or, therefore, however** or **nevertheless.**) They test a sentence like, **They were tired _____ they went on a trip.** Note that the words that follow the blank are a complete sentence. Any word that fits in the blank and that renders the sentence sensible is a conjunction. Students identify those words: They were tired **when** they went on a trip; they were tired **because** they went on a trip; they were tired **until** they went on a trip; etc. Students make up different sentences that use the various words. The process of testing is very powerful. Reinforce it. If you substitute a word that does the same thing as the original word, both words have the same part of speech.

In lesson 72, teams create an extended outline diagram to write a passage that is at least five paragraphs long. Different members of a team write different parts, which are critiqued by the team and then incorporated into the team's account.

Teams present their work to the class in the following lesson; they revise their accounts based on feedback.

In lesson 74, students identify the problem with a test for determining whether boys in a classroom are taller than girls. The conclusion drawn by the argument is that boys are taller. This evidence was based on the four tallest 10-year-olds in a classroom. (Three of those students are boys.) Students make up a class list of 26 students. They show the height and sex of each student. They arrange the heights so that their data meet two requirements: 1) Three of the four tallest students are boys; 2) Their listing of heights clearly shows that the girls are taller than the boys. Teams then write an argument that critiques the original argument by referring to the team-constructed data.

In lesson 75, the teams report to the class. The teams edit their arguments, based on class feedback.

In lesson 76, teams revisit the conjunctions that they identified to find those that are always nonessential. They conclude that a conjunction is always part of a nonessential clause if they cannot identify a clause in which it is essential. They later test their conclusions by referring to a reference book on usage or grammar.

In lesson 77, teams deal with an argument that may present a false dilemma. Teams identify a test that would provide adequate data to show whether the original conclusion is correct or whether other possible explanations for the outcome are more reasonable. This activity, like the others, is presented in phases. After students work out a good test, they develop an outline diagram for presenting their critique. Then they write the critique and present it to the class. Again, revisions follow feedback (lesson 78).

In lesson 79 is another example of a conclusion that may be a false dilemma. Students determine that the conclusion is misleading by combining information from different sources. The conclusion of the original argument is that safety regulations in Tintown are not effective because the number of accidents has gone up since these regulations were introduced. The argument is accompanied by a graph that supports the conclusion.

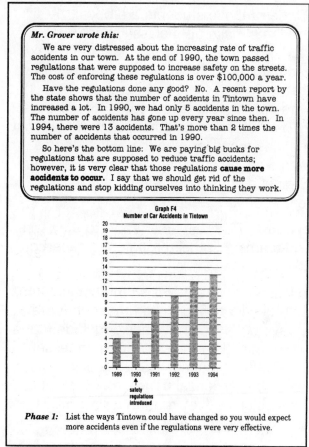

Mr. Grover wrote this:

We are very distressed about the increasing rate of traffic accidents in our town. At the end of 1990, the town passed regulations that were supposed to increase safety on the streets. The cost of enforcing these regulations is over $100,000 a year.

Have the regulations done any good? No. A recent report by the state shows that the number of accidents in Tintown have increased a lot. In 1990, we had only 5 accidents in the town. The number of accidents has gone up every year since then. In 1994, there were 13 accidents. That's more than 2 times the number of accidents that occurred in 1990.

So here's the bottom line: We are paying big bucks for regulations that are supposed to reduce traffic accidents; however, it is very clear that those regulations **cause more accidents to occur.** I say that we should get rid of the regulations and stop kidding ourselves into thinking they work.

Graph F4
Number of Car Accidents in Tintown

Phase 1: List the ways Tintown could have changed so you would expect more accidents even if the regulations were very effective.

Teams combine this information with information about the number of miles driven in Tintown.

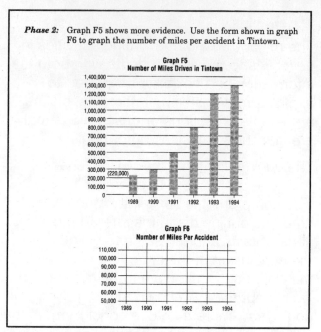

Phase 2: Graph F5 shows more evidence. Use the form shown in graph F6 to graph the number of miles per accident in Tintown.

Graph F5
Number of Miles Driven in Tintown

Graph F6
Number of Miles Per Accident

They derive data that is similar to data they used in several earlier exercises: number per number. Here's the table they develop:

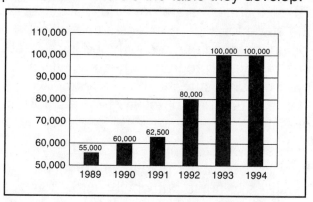

Teams then write about the problem and draw the conclusion that the regulations are effective.

The work integrates math, science and writing into the fabric of thinking. Students apply logical tests. They think logically. More important, they write in a way that shows their thoughts clearly.

With this start, you can present students with exercises that use reference books and that involve numbers and possibilities. Students should be able to deal with the concepts and express them in language that is clear and stylistically acceptable.

Writing Extensions

The Writing Extensions in lessons 81–100 consist of 20 scripted lessons and 10 blackline masters (BLMs). Each extension activity requires between 20–30 minutes.

The general objective of the extensions is to give students opportunities to apply what they have learned about writing to a wider variety of contexts. Students should be able to write the various essays that the extensions present with a minimum of additional teaching or preparation. In addition to the activities specified for extensions, you may elect to give students additional assignments that require them to compare and contrast or to debate different issues. These assignments follow the same format as the assignments presented in the extensions.

This work on less-structured assignments also prepares the students for tests that require writing and that give students only general directions.

Two types of activities are presented in the 20 extension lessons. One type requires students to retell accounts that are fairly involved. For the other type of activities, students write five-paragraph essays.

RETELL

The extension presents 10 retell activities. The format for Retells is far less structured than it is in the regular program. The students are assumed to be able to retell adequately when structure is provided. The retell activities in the extension do not present vocabulary words, do not direct students to take notes, and do not provide for the prompting of any content that they are to retell. There are no BLMs for Retells. You read the passage to the students twice. Then students write it as accurately as they can.

Do not introduce more structure unless students tend to flounder. If they do not preform well on a retell assignment, tell them that they may take notes if they wish, and that if they failed to remember important things, they should take notes. Do not, however, make note-taking a mandatory activity or a part of the retell routine that they follow.

Handle spelling in the same as-needed basis. If students ask about the spelling of a word, tell them how to spell it. If they ask about a word meaning, tell them the meaning. But do not offer this information.

After students hand in their accounts, mark the problems and return the papers to the students. Indicate where they left out important information. Students then rewrite their essay. You may choose to have students illustrate their finished papers. If students generally did not perform well on the assignment, tell them to look over places that you have marked on their Retell. Then repeat the exercise.

FIVE-PARAGRAPH ESSAYS

The extension presents 10 five-paragraph essay assignments. Each has a BLM that provides a written scenario and the essay's objectives. The first two five-paragraph assignments also show the outline diagram students are to follow. After these lessons (lessons 84 and 85), students are expected to write the five-paragraph essays without referring to the outline diagram.

The first four essays are persuasive arguments. Students assume a particular viewpoint and present reasons that lead to a particular conclusion. They attempt to make their argument compelling, supported by reasons and persuasive language.

For the next three essays, students compare and contrast. For the last three essays, students write how-to directions.

To present each essay, pass out the BLM for the lesson. Reproducible BLMs appear in the teacher's *Presentation Book*. The number of the BLM corresponds to the extension lesson number. The first five-paragraph essay occurs in lesson 84. It is labeled BLM84. Read the BLM to the students. Then direct them to write their essay. If they do not finish it in class, assign it as homework. You may elect to present some of the other five-paragraph essays as homework.

SEQUENCE

Below is the sequence of activities for the writing extensions. Note that the schedule alternates between presenting lessons that involve retelling and lessons that involve five-paragraph essays.

Extension	81	82	83	84	85	86	87	88	89	90	91	92	93	94	95	96	97	98	99	100
Retell	✔	✔	✔			✔	✔			✔		✔		✔		✔		✔		
Essay				✔	✔			✔	✔		✔		✔		✔		✔		✔	✔
BLM				✔	✔			✔	✔		✔		✔		✔		✔		✔	✔
Rewrite	✔	✔	✔			✔	✔			✔	✔	✔	✔	✔	✔	✔	✔	✔	✔	✔

Tests

In-Program Tests

The in-program tests that appear as every tenth lesson of the program provide a basis for periodically judging the progress of individual students and for awarding grades.

During a test, students should be seated so that they cannot "copy."

Directions for presenting and scoring the test appear as part of each test lesson.

When observing students' performance, make sure that they are following directions, but do not tell them answers to any item or give them hints.

Mark each item a student misses on the test.

Count the number of mistakes and enter the number at the top of each student's test.

Before returning the test forms, use your copy of the reproducible Group Summary sheets that appear on pages 105 and 106 and enter the number of errors each student made.

Scoring the Tests

Scoring guidelines are specified as part of each test lesson. Unless noted, spelling and basic grammar (e.g., capitals, end marks) are not part of the scoring criteria.

The number of points possible for each test varies from test to test.

The number indicating points possible should guide scoring. For example:

- Count as errors any mistake that relates to **what was taught** in the lesson relevant to that part.

- **Spelling** is not taught, so generally, do not count off for spelling. However, on some occasions correct spelling is expected. For example, if the words on the student textbook page only need to be copied, they should be spelled correctly. Another occasion is when two words are given and the student must write a contraction. The contraction must be spelled correctly.
- Meaning is a focus of the program. Sometimes spelling affects the meaning. If the meaning is wrong, then the item is wrong. *Word endings* and *verb tense* changes affect meaning. These kinds of errors count.

If you are teaching spelling in another sequence of lessons, you can hold a student accountable for transferring their spelling and basic grammar to their writing by doing such things as:

1. Asking students to rewrite the sentences or passages with no spelling or grammar errors in order for the grade to be recorded (i.e., the score assumes perfect spelling so "fix it so it is perfect to get the score.").
2. Adding points possible for each test for additional expectations.

Test Remedies

Test remedies are specified as part of each test lesson (under the heading **Test Remedies**). The criterion for determining whether or not students need a remedy is the percentage of students that makes mistakes on a particular part of the test. The criteria are specified as part of the test lesson. Typically, the criteria are stated like this:

If more than 1/4 of the students made 2 or more errors in part __, present the following exercises. (A list of exercises follows.)

The remedies indicate what you should do if the class has problems; however, the guidelines for providing remedies are quite general. Here are more specific guidelines.

1. If students perform poorly on a test, they will probably have trouble on later exercises in the program and should be given a remedy before the next lesson is presented.

2. In many classrooms, the same students tend to perform poorly on different tests; if those are the only students who perform poorly, do not present the remedy to the entire class. If possible, present the remedy to only the students who need it.

3. If it's not possible to schedule a time for providing the remedy to a small group of students (and not the entire class), give the students who performed well a writing assignment similar to the ones on the lessons preceding the test. As they work on the assignment, present the remedies to the students who need additional help.

4. If more than one-fourth of the students have trouble with a part of the test, present the remedy for that part to all students. Then present the lesson that follows the test.

5. If more than one-fourth of students repeatedly make an unacceptably high number of errors on the tests, try to analyze what's wrong. Possibly, the students should not be placed in Level F. Possibly, they are not trying very hard.

6. Use effective enforcement practices to prompt harder work and better performance. A good guide is *The Solution Book* by Randall Sprick. This text, published by SRA, contains specific suggestions for increasing student motivation.

Objectives

The objectives show the development of skills and operations taught in *Reasoning and Writing, Level F.*

The skills and operations are grouped by tracks. The headings indicate the major tracks and the divisions within each track. Each track shows the development of a major topic, such as parts of speech and sentence analysis or passage writing. Typically, a track will have activities that are presented over many different lessons of the program.

The major tracks are:

RETELL
GRAMMAR AND USAGE
GENERAL/SPECIFIC
CLARITY OF MEANING
DEDUCTION AND INFERENCES
WRITING
WRITING EXTENSIONS

Within each track there are divisions. Each division is marked by a subheading.

The subheadings for Grammar and Usage are:

SENTENCES
NOUNS
PRONOUNS
ADJECTIVES
VERBS
VERB TENSE AGREEMENT
ADVERBS
USING ADVERBS AND ADJECTIVES
    CORRECTLY
PARALLELISM
POSSESSIVES
SUBJECT-VERB AGREEMENT
PASSIVE TO ACTIVE
TEAM ACTIVITY PROJECTS

The subheadings for Clarity of Meaning are:

COMPARATIVES
DESCRIPTIONS
ESSENTIAL AND NONESSENTIAL
    ELEMENTS
AMBIGUOUS ADJECTIVES
AMBIGUOUS VERBS

Although the objectives show the various categories and the lessons in which each specific objective is taught, the objectives do not show the interrelationships among the various skills. Specific skills are involved in more than one track. For instance, students learn to replace unclear pronouns with clear nouns in sentence-type activities. This skill is utilized in the editing activities, where students rewrite poorly written passages, and is utilized again in extended critique activities as students explain the problems with arguments.

In summary, the objectives show the various skills and operations that are taught; however, skills and operations developed in one track invariably spill over into other tracks as students use and apply what they have learned.

	OBJECTIVES	LESSONS
Retell	Take notes and reconstruct a dictated passage.	7, 8, 16, 17, 37, 47, 49, 54

Grammar and Usage

	OBJECTIVES	LESSONS
Sentences	Discriminate between sentences and partial sentences.	1
	Identify when the word **that** is a conjunction.	69
Nouns	Test whether words are nouns by applying the one-or-some test.	1, 2
	Test the last word in a sentence to determine whether it is a noun.	3, 4
Pronouns	Replace nouns at the end of sentences with appropriate pronouns.	5
	Replace pronouns in sentences with acceptable noun phrases (adjectives with nouns).	6, 7
	Label the parts of speech in combined sentences that have a relative pronoun.	66
	Rewrite sentences that refer to an indefinite **they.**	67
Adjectives	Transform sentences that end with an adjective into parallel sentences that end with a noun.	8
	Apply the rule that verbs of the senses use adjectives, not adverbs.	53, 54
	Rewrite sentences that use the adjective **this** or **that** without a noun.	64–66
Verbs	Identify the number of actors that a verb refers to.	12, 14, 15
	Identify the tense for verbs.	13–15
	Indicate both the number of actors and the tense for verbs in sentences.	16, 18
	Discriminate between verbs and words that are not verbs.	17
	Identify verbs and their tense.	19, 21, 23
	Discriminate verbs from non-verbs (verbals).	28
Verb Tense Agreement	Write sentences that refer to phenomena that are always true.	24, 25
	Edit a narrative passage so that all the sentences are written in the past tense.	26
	Rewrite sentences with the verbs **can** and **will** so they tell about past time.	27
	Rewrite sentences that refer to the present so that they refer to the past.	29, 31
	Rewrite present-tense sentences that have direct quotes so they tell about past time.	34

	OBJECTIVES	LESSONS
USING CRITERIA TO MAKE DECISIONS	Follow an outline diagram to critique a decision that is based on multiple criteria.	2, 5
	Follow an outline diagram to make a decision based on multiple criteria.	3
MORE GENERAL CONCLUSIONS	Follow an outline diagram to write about arguments that have a conclusion that is more general than the evidence.	6, 7, 11
Ambiguous Meanings	Follow an outline diagram to describe the silly meaning of sentences that are not perfectly parallel.	14, 15, 21
Unclear Directions	Follow an outline diagram to describe the problems with a set of directions.	41–44
	Follow an outline diagram to describe the problems with directions for making figures.	45, 46
Misleading Information **INDIVIDUAL-GROUP FALLACIES**	Identify rules that could be discredited by finding one individual who does not follow the rule.	23, 24
	Discriminate sentences that tell about every individual in a group from sentences that tell about the group as a unit.	25
	Follow an outline diagram to write about flaws in arguments that involve individuals and groups.	26–28
PART-WHOLE FALLACIES	Follow an outline diagram to describe part-whole fallacies.	61, 62
MISLEADING STATISTICS	Follow an outline diagram to identify the problems with arguments that present statistical information.	66–69
Comparing and Synthesizing Information **COMPARE AND CONTRAST**	Follow outline diagrams to organize comparison information two ways.	16–19
IDENTIFYING RELIABLE SOURCES	Indicate which of two possible sources answers questions.	37, 38, 45, 46, 56
	Follow an outline diagram to identify a reliable source that answers a question.	45
SYNTHESIZING INFORMATION	Follow an outline diagram to resolve an inconsistency in reports.	55
	Follow an outline diagram to write a paragraph that explains how two things are the same.	63
SIMILES	Write general sentences that tell how two things are the same.	51, 52, 55
	Follow an outline diagram to write pairs of parallel sentences that explain how two things are the same.	56, 57, 59

	OBJECTIVES	LESSONS
ANALOGIES	Follow an outline diagram to explain parallel features that are opposite.	53
Rule Generating, Rule Testing, and Consistency RULE TESTING	Indicate plausible antecedent events.	8
	Follow an outline diagram to describe a reasonable test for a rule.	9, 11, 12
	Follow an outline diagram to discredit rules.	14
	Follow an outline diagram to write a paragraph that indicates what kind of test is needed to confirm or discredit a statement about a group.	22
REVISING RULES BASED ON NEW EVIDENCE	Construct rules that are consistent with a set of examples. Then follow an outline diagram to describe why one example discredits the rules.	18
	Follow an outline diagram to discredit rules based on a large set of examples.	19
	Follow an outline diagram and use data about concrete examples to determine a probable rule.	57
NOTING INCONSISTENCIES AND CONTRADICTIONS	Follow an outline diagram to write a paragraph that points out inconsistencies between a table and a conclusion based on the table.	21–24
	Follow an outline diagram to explain an inconsistency.	32
	Use information given in a table and follow an outline diagram to write about inconsistent features of an object.	34
	Follow an outline diagram to describe inconsistencies in reports.	35, 36
	Follow an outline diagram to describe contradictions in reports.	39
	Identify whether passages are inconsistent or contradictory.	39, 49
	Follow an outline diagram to explain how an account contradicts a graph.	41, 42, 48
	Follow an outline diagram to explain how one account contradicts another.	43
	Follow an outline diagram to correct an inaccuracy.	44, 51–54
	Follow an outline diagram to explain how an account contradicts an important detail of another account.	46
	Follow an outline diagram to write about features of an object that are inconsistent with information given in a table.	47

OBJECTIVES		LESSONS
	Write and punctuate sentences that have a nonessential clause.	33–35
	Use the words **that** or **which** to combine sentences.	36, 37
	Write combined sentences that have the words **who, that** or **which.**	38
Ambiguous Adjectives	Rewrite sentences that present more than one phrase in an ambiguous order.	64, 65
Ambiguous Verbs	Rewrite sentences that have an unclear verb.	66–68

Deductions and Inferences

OBJECTIVES		LESSONS
Drawing Conclusions from Evidence	Write conclusions for deductions.	1, 2
Discrediting Rules	Determine whether observations of different populations support or discredit a rule.	4, 5
	Respond to a series of questions about discrediting a rule.	6, 7
	Respond to a series of questions about discrediting a parallel rule.	6
	Determine which examples a rule refers to and whether any of the examples to discredit the rule.	13
	Follow an outline diagram to discredit rules.	14, 19
Constructing Rules from Observations	Construct rules that are consistent with a set of examples.	15–18
Consistency	Indicate which possibility is most consistent with a set of facts.	25
	Use picture information to make a group of graded objects consistent with information about one of the objects.	27
	Complete a table with facts that are consistent with given information.	28, 29
	Complete a table with information that is consistent with facts already present in the table.	31, 33

Writing

OBJECTIVES		LESSONS
Critiquing WRONG CONCLUSIONS	Follow an outline diagram to write about the problems with arguments that draw improper conclusions.	1
	Follow the appropriate outline diagram to write about the problems with arguments that draw improper conclusions.	14
Invalid Arguments OTHER POSSIBILITIES	Follow an outline diagram to critique arguments that draw one of many possible conclusions.	2–4, 9, 12

	OBJECTIVES	LESSONS
USING CRITERIA TO MAKE DECISIONS	Follow an outline diagram to critique a decision that is based on multiple criteria.	2, 5
	Follow an outline diagram to make a decision based on multiple criteria.	3
MORE GENERAL CONCLUSIONS	Follow an outline diagram to write about arguments that have a conclusion that is more general than the evidence.	6, 7, 11
Ambiguous Meanings	Follow an outline diagram to describe the silly meaning of sentences that are not perfectly parallel.	14, 15, 21
Unclear Directions	Follow an outline diagram to describe the problems with a set of directions.	41–44
	Follow an outline diagram to describe the problems with directions for making figures.	45, 46
Misleading Information **INDIVIDUAL-GROUP FALLACIES**	Identify rules that could be discredited by finding one individual who does not follow the rule.	23, 24
	Discriminate sentences that tell about every individual in a group from sentences that tell about the group as a unit.	25
	Follow an outline diagram to write about flaws in arguments that involve individuals and groups.	26–28
PART-WHOLE FALLACIES	Follow an outline diagram to describe part-whole fallacies.	61, 62
MISLEADING STATISTICS	Follow an outline diagram to identify the problems with arguments that present statistical information.	66–69
Comparing and Synthesizing Information **COMPARE AND CONTRAST**	Follow outline diagrams to organize comparison information two ways.	16–19
IDENTIFYING RELIABLE SOURCES	Indicate which of two possible sources answers questions.	37, 38, 45, 46, 56
	Follow an outline diagram to identify a reliable source that answers a question.	45
SYNTHESIZING INFORMATION	Follow an outline diagram to resolve an inconsistency in reports.	55
	Follow an outline diagram to write a paragraph that explains how two things are the same.	63
SIMILES	Write general sentences that tell how two things are the same.	51, 52, 55
	Follow an outline diagram to write pairs of parallel sentences that explain how two things are the same.	56, 57, 59

	OBJECTIVES	LESSONS
ANALOGIES	Follow an outline diagram to explain parallel features that are opposite.	53
Rule Generating, Rule Testing, and Consistency **RULE TESTING**	Indicate plausible antecedent events.	8
	Follow an outline diagram to describe a reasonable test for a rule.	9, 11, 12
	Follow an outline diagram to discredit rules.	14
	Follow an outline diagram to write a paragraph that indicates what kind of test is needed to confirm or discredit a statement about a group.	22
REVISING RULES BASED ON NEW EVIDENCE	Construct rules that are consistent with a set of examples. Then follow an outline diagram to describe why one example discredits the rules.	18
	Follow an outline diagram to discredit rules based on a large set of examples.	19
	Follow an outline diagram and use data about concrete examples to determine a probable rule.	57
NOTING INCONSISTENCIES AND CONTRADICTIONS	Follow an outline diagram to write a paragraph that points out inconsistencies between a table and a conclusion based on the table.	21–24
	Follow an outline diagram to explain an inconsistency.	32
	Use information given in a table and follow an outline diagram to write about inconsistent features of an object.	34
	Follow an outline diagram to describe inconsistencies in reports.	35, 36
	Follow an outline diagram to describe contradictions in reports.	39
	Identify whether passages are inconsistent or contradictory.	39, 49
	Follow an outline diagram to explain how an account contradicts a graph.	41, 42, 48
	Follow an outline diagram to explain how one account contradicts another.	43
	Follow an outline diagram to correct an inaccuracy.	44, 51–54
	Follow an outline diagram to explain how an account contradicts an important detail of another account.	46
	Follow an outline diagram to write about features of an object that are inconsistent with information given in a table.	47

OBJECTIVES		LESSONS
DESIGNING EXPERIMENTS	Follow an outline diagram to describe a test that would confirm or discredit a rule.	58, 59
FALSE CAUSE	Follow an outline diagram to describe fallacies involving false cause.	61–65

Team Activity Projects

Identify new conjunctions and write an argument that tells why they are conjunctions.	71
Construct an outline diagram that explains the problems with an argument.	72
Follow an outline diagram and write a passage that explains the problems with an argument.	73
Create a larger sample of evidence to show why a smaller sample may not be fair. Design an outline diagram for writing about the problem with the evidence and write the critique.	74
Revise and edit a report.	75
Determine if a conjunction introduces a part that is always **nonessential.**	76
Identify other possible explanations for evidence. Design a test for each of those possibilities, and write about what the different possible outcomes would mean.	77, 78
Evaluate and critique a misleading argument by presenting the evidence in a fair way and writing a critique.	79, 80

Writing Extensions

Retell	Reconstruct a dictated account.	81–83, 86, 87, 90, 92, 94, 96, 98
5-Paragraph Essays	Follow an outline diagram to write a persuasive 5-paragraph essay	84, 85
	Write a persuasive 5-paragraph essay.	88, 89
	Research and write a 5-paragraph comparison essay.	91, 93, 95
	Research and write a [5-paragraph] how-to account.	97, 99, 100
Rewrite	Rewrite [and illustrate] the account	81–83, 86, 87, 90–100

Skills Profile—Page 1

The charts on pages 99 to 104 may be reproduced to make a skills profile for each student. The charts summarize the skills presented in *Reasoning and Writing F* and provide space for indicating the date on which the student completes the lessons in which the skills are taught.

Student's name _____   Grade or year in school _____

Teacher's name _____

Starting lesson _____   Date _____

Last lesson completed _____   Date _____   Number of days absent _____

Skills	Taught in These Lessons	Date Lessons Completed	Skills	Taught in These Lessons	Date Lessons Completed
RETELL Take notes and reconstruct a dictated passage.	7–54		**Adjectives** Transform sentences that end with an adjective into parallel sentences that end with a noun.	8	
GRAMMAR AND USAGE **Sentences** Discriminate between sentences and partial sentences.	1		Apply the rule that verbs of the senses use adjectives, not adverbs.	53, 54	
Identify when the word **that** is a conjunction.	69		Rewrite sentences that use the adjective **this** or **that** without a noun	64–66	
Nouns Test whether words are nouns by applying the one-or-some test.	1, 2		**Verbs** Identify the number of actors that a verb refers to.	12, 14, 15	
Test the last word in a sentence to determine whether it is a noun.	3, 4		Identify the tense for verbs.	13–15	
Pronouns Replace nouns at the end of sentences with appropriate pronouns.	5		Indicate both the number of actors and the tense for verbs in sentences.	16, 18	
Replace pronouns in sentences with acceptable noun phrases (adjectives with nouns).	6, 7		Discriminate between verbs and words that are not verbs.	17	
Label the parts of speech in combined sentences that have a relative pronoun.	66		Identity verbs and their tense.	19–23	
Rewrite sentences that refer to an indefinite **they.**	67		Discriminate verbs from non-verbs (verbals).	28	
			Verb Tense Agreement Write sentences that refer to phenomena that are always true.	24, 25	
			Edit a narrative passage so that all the sentences are written in the past tense.	26	

Skills Profile—Page 2   Name_____

Skills	Taught in These Lessons	Date Lessons Completed	Skills	Taught in These Lessons	Date Lessons Completed
Rewrite sentences with the verbs **can** and **will** so they tell about past time.	27		**Possessives** Discriminate between singular and plural possessives.	35, 36	
Rewrite sentences that refer to the present so that they refer to the past.	29, 31		Rewrite sentences that have possessive nouns so they refer to the ____ of ____ .	38–41	
Write past-tense sentences that have a present-tense clause.	32, 33		**Subject-Verb Agreement** Indicate the correct verb by referring to the number indicated by the subject of the sentence.	51–56	
Rewrite present-tense sentences that have direct quotes so they tell about past time.	34		Identify the main noun and generate the verb in sentences of the form: **The group of campers ( ) resting.**	56, 57	
Adverbs Identify adverbs at the end of sentences.	31, 32		Rewrite sentences that have a subject with the word **of**.	**58, 59**	
Discriminate between sentences that end with an adjective and sentences that end with an adverb.	33		**Passive to Active** Transform passive-voice sentences into active-voice sentences.	61–63	
Using Adverbs and Adjectives Correctly Indicate whether verbs are **is** verbs.	41, 42		Edit a passage that contains passive-voice sentences.	64, 65	
Use the appropriate word to complete a pair of sentences that differs only in the verb.	42–44		**Cumulative** Identify nouns, pronouns and adjectives in sentences.	11–19	
Change sentences that end with an adjective so they end with an adverb.	45, 46		Discriminate between adverbs, adjectives and nouns.	35–39	
Discriminate between adverbs and adjectives.	47, 52		Edit a passage that has different types of problems.	58–68	
Parallelism Construct sentences that are increasingly more parallel than the original sentence.	48		**GENERAL/SPECIFIC** **More General—More Specific** Compare similar statements and indicate which statement is more general.	1	
Construct compound sentences that have parallel parts.	49, 51		Compare similar statements and indicate which statement is more specific.	2	
Rewrite sentences that fail to use parallel lists.	61, 62		Combine subjects and predicates of two sentences to create a sentence more specific than either sentence shown.	2	
Rewrite sentences that do not have parallel lists. Make them more than one sentence.	63				

Skills	Taught in These Lessons	Date Lessons Completed	Skills	Taught in These Lessons	Date Lessons Completed
Combine subjects and predicates of three sentences to create a sentence more specific than any of the sentences shown.	3		Write a pair of sentences, one more specific than the original and one more general than the original.	25	
Determine whether the conclusion of an argument is more general or more specific than the evidence.	4, 5		**Essential and Nonessential Elements** Identify whether the word **who** or the word **that** is appropriate.	25	
Write both general and specific answers to pairs of questions.	6		Combine pairs of sentences into a single sentence that uses the word **who** or **that**.	25, 26	
Definitions Write nonessential clauses that describe or define.	41–43		Use picture information to add essential wording that begins with **who** or **that**.	27–32	
Appositives Write sentences that have an appositive that describes an unfamiliar word.	44, 45		Write and punctuate sentences that have a nonessential clause.	33–35	
Appropriate Category Words Describe unfamiliar words in sentences by adding category words.	48–51		Use the words **that** or **which** to combine sentences.	36, 37	
Complete sentences that describe an unfamiliar word by indicating only the category for the word.	52–55		Write combined sentences that have the words **who, that** or **which**.	38	
CLARITY OF MEANING **Comparatives** Use the wording in a comparison sentence to create parallel wording.	7, 8		**Ambiguous Adjectives** Rewrite sentences that present more than one phrase in an ambiguous order.	64, 65	
Identify whether comparison sentences have a silly meaning when they are made more parallel.	9–12		**Ambiguous Verbs** Rewrite sentences that have an unclear verb.	66–68	
Identify the silly meanings of sentences.	13		**DEDUCTIONS AND INFERENCES** **Drawing Conclusions from Evidence** Write conclusions for deductions.	1, 2	
Descriptions Rewrite statements so they are specific enough to tell about a designated object.	21		**Discrediting Rules** Determine whether observations of different populations support or discredit a rule.	4, 5	
Write questions that describe differences about a designated object.	22		Respond to a series of questions about discrediting a rule.	6, 7	
Make sentences specific enough to tell about only one of two pictures.	23–26		Respond to a series of questions about discrediting a parallel rule.	6	
Make sentences general enough to tell about only one of two pictures.	24		Determine which examples a rule refers to and whether any of the examples discredit the rule.	13	
			Follow an outline diagram to discredit rules.	14, 19	

Skills	Taught in These Lessons	Date Lessons Completed	Skills	Taught in These Lessons	Date Lessons Completed
Constructing Rules from Observations			**Ambiguous Meanings**		
Construct rules that are consistent with a set of examples.	15–18		Follow an outline diagram to describe the silly meaning of sentences that are not perfectly parallel.	14–21	
Consistency			**Unclear Directions**		
Indicate which possibility is most consistent with a set of facts.	25		Follow an outline diagram to describe problems with a set of directions.	41–44	
Use picture information to make a group of graded objects consistent with information about one of the objects.	27		Follow an outline diagram to describe the problems with directions for making figures.	45, 46	
Complete a table with facts that are consistent with given information.	28, 29		**Misleading Information**		
Complete a table with information that is consistent with facts already present in the table.	31, 33		**INDIVIDUAL-GROUP FALLACIES** Identify rules that could be discredited by finding one individual who does not follow the rule.	23, 24	
WRITING **Critiquing** **WRONG CONCLUSIONS** Follow an outline diagram to write about the problems with arguments that draw improper conclusions.	1		Discriminate sentences that tell about every individual in a group from sentences that tell about the group as a unit.	25	
Follow the appropriate outline diagram to write about the problems with arguments that draw improper conclusions.	14		Follow an outline diagram to write about flaws in arguments that involve individuals and groups.	26–28	
Invalid Arguments **OTHER POSSIBILITIES** Follow an outline diagram to critique arguments that draw one of many possible conclusions.	2–12		**PART-WHOLE FALLACIES** Follow an outline diagram to describe part-whole fallacies.	61, 62	
USING CRITERIA TO MAKE DECISIONS Follow an outline diagram to critique a decision that is based on multiple criteria.	2, 5		**MISLEADING STATISTICS** Follow an outline diagram to identify problems with arguments that present statistical information.	66–69	
Follow an outline diagram to make a decision based on multiple criteria.	3		**Comparing and Synthesizing Information** **COMPARE AND CONTRAST** Follow outline diagrams to organize comparison information two ways.	16–19	
MORE GENERAL CONCLUSIONS Follow an outline diagram to write about arguments that have a conclusion that is more general than the evidence.	6–11		**IDENTIFYING RELIABLE SOURCES** Indicate which of two possible sources answers questions.	37–56	
			Follow an outline diagram to identify a reliable source that answers a question.	45	

Skills	Taught in These Lessons	Date Lessons Completed	Skills	Taught in These Lessons	Date Lessons Completed
SYNTHESIZING INFORMATION			**NOTING INCONSISTENCIES AND CONTRADICTIONS**		
Follow an outline diagram to resolve an inconsistency in reports.	55		Follow an outline diagram to write a paragraph that points out inconsistencies between a table and a conclusion based on the table.	21–24	
Follow an outline diagram to write paragraph that explains how two things are the same.	63		Follow an outline diagram to explain an inconsistency.	32	
SIMILES			Use information given in a table and follow an outline diagram to write about inconsistent features of an object.	34	
Write general sentences that tell how two things are the same.	51–55				
Follow an outline diagram to write pairs of parallel sentences that explain how two things are the same.	56–59		Follow an outline diagram to describe inconsistencies in reports.	35, 36	
ANALOGIES			Follow an outline diagram to describe contradictions in reports.	39	
Follow an outline diagram to explain parallel features that are opposite.	53		Identify whether passages are inconsistent or contradictory.	39, 49	
Rule Generating, Rule Testing, and Consistency			Follow an outline diagram to explain how an account contradicts a graph.	41–48	
RULE TESTING					
Indicate plausible antecedent events.	8		Follow an outline diagram to explain how one account contradicts another.	43	
Follow an outline diagram to describe a reasonable test for a rule.	9–12		Follow an outline diagram to correct an inaccuracy.	44–54	
Follow an outline diagram to discredit rules.	14		Follow an outline diagram to explain how an account contradicts an important detail of another account.	46	
Follow an outline diagram to write a paragraph that indicates what kind of test is needed to confirm or discredit a statement about a group.	22		Follow an outline diagram to write about features of an object that are inconsistent with information given in a table.	47	
REVISING RULES BASED ON NEW EVIDENCE					
Construct rules that are consistent with a set of examples. Then follow an outline diagram to describe why one example discredits the rules.	18		**DESIGNING EXPERIMENTS**		
Follow an outline diagram to discredit rules based on a large set of examples.	19		Follow an outline diagram to describe a test that would confirm or discredit a rule.	58, 59	
Follow an outline diagram and use data about concrete examples to determine a probable rule.	57		**FALSE CAUSE**		
			Follow an outline diagram to describe fallacies involving false cause.	61–65	

Skills	Taught in These Lessons	Date Lessons Completed	Skills	Taught in These Lessons	Date Lessons Completed
TEAM ACTIVITY PROJECTS			**Writing Extensions**		
			Retell		
Identify new conjunctions and write an argument that tells why they are conjunctions.	71		Reconstruct a dictated account.	81–98	
			5-Paragraph Essays		
Construct an outline diagram that explains the problems with an argument.	72		Follow an outline diagram to write a persuasive 5-paragraph essay.	84, 85	
Follow an outline diagram and write a passage that explains the problems with an argument.	73		Write a persuasive 5-paragraph essay	88, 89	
Create a larger sample of evidence to show why a smaller sample may not be fair. Design an outline diagram for writing about the problem with the evidence and write the critique.	74		Research and write a 5-paragraph comparison essay.	91–95	
			Research and write a [5-paragraph] how-to account.	97–100	
Revise and edit a report.	75		**Rewrite**		
Determine if a conjunction introduces a part that is always **nonessential.**	76		Rewrite [and illustrate] the account	81–100	
Identify other possible explanations for evidence. Design a test for each of those possibilities, and write about what the different possible outcomes would mean.	77, 78				
Evaluate and critique a misleading argument by presenting the evidence in a fair way and writing a critique.	79, 80				

Group Summary of Test Performance

Note: Test scoring guidelines and test remedies are specified in the teacher's Presentation Book.

Name

	Test 1: 30 pts					Test 2: 43 pts			Test 3: 20 pts			
	X parts not passed					**X** parts not passed			**X** parts not passed			
	A	B	C	D	E	A	B	C	A	B	C	D
1												
2												
3												
4												
5												
6												
7												
8												
9												
10												
11												
12												
13												
14												
15												
16												
17												
18												
19												
20												
21												
22												
23												
24												
25												
26												
27												
28												
29												
30												
Number of students not Passed = NP												
Total number of students = T												
Remedy needed if NP/T = 25% or more												

Group Summary of Test Performance

Note: Test scoring guidelines and test remedies are specified in the teacher's Presentation Book.

Name	Test 4: 24 pts X parts not passed				Test 5: 30 pts X parts not passed				Test 6: 30 pts X parts not passed					Test 7: 28 pts X parts not passed			
	A	B	C	D	A	B	C	D	A	B	C	D	E	A	B	C	D
1																	
2																	
3																	
4																	
5																	
6																	
7																	
8																	
9																	
10																	
11																	
12																	
13																	
14																	
15																	
16																	
17																	
18																	
19																	
20																	
21																	
22																	
23																	
24																	
25																	
26																	
27																	
28																	
29																	
30																	
Number of students not Passed = NP																	
Total number of students = T																	
Remedy needed if NP/T = 25% or more																	